OCS Study
MMS 2001-057

Coastal Marine Institute

Investigation of Pressure and Pressure Gradients along the Louisiana/Texas Inner Shelf and Their Relationships to Wind Forcing and Current Variability

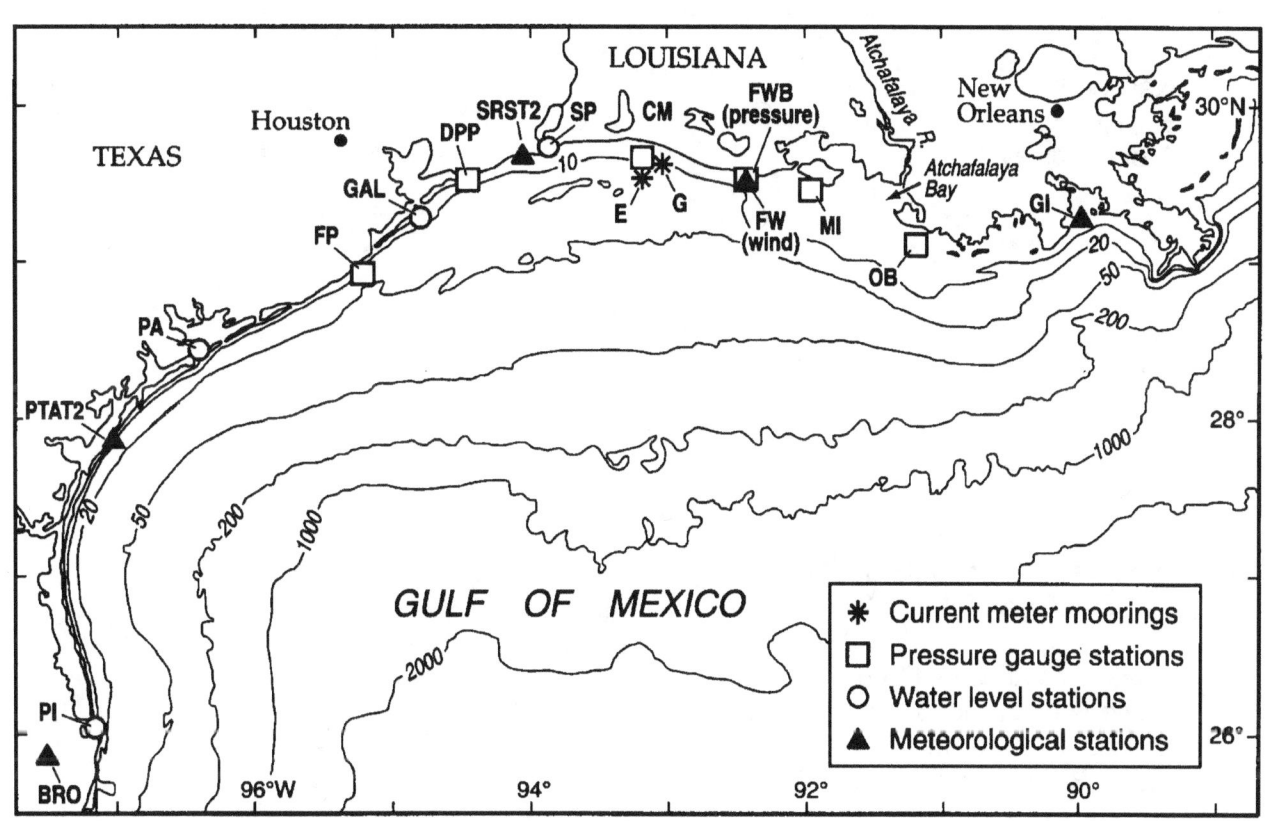

U.S. Department of the Interior
Minerals Management Service
Gulf of Mexico OCS Region

Cooperative Agreement
Coastal Marine Institute
Louisiana State University

OCS Study
MMS 2001-057

Coastal Marine Institute

Investigation of Pressure and Pressure Gradients along the Louisiana/Texas Inner Shelf and Their Relationships to Wind Forcing and Current Variability

Authors

Nan Walker
Ewa Jarosz
Steve Murray

August 2001

Prepared under MMS Contract
14-35-0001-30660-19922
by
Coastal Studies Institute
Howe-Russell Geoscience Complex
Louisiana State University
Baton Rouge, Louisiana 70801

Published by

U.S. Department of the Interior
Minerals Management Service
Gulf of Mexico OCS Region

Cooperative Agreement
Coastal Marine Institute
Louisiana State University

DISCLAIMER

This report was prepared under contract between the Minerals Management Service (MMS) and Coastal Studies Institute, Louisiana State University. This report has been technically reviewed by the MMS and approved for publication. Approval does not signify that the contents necessarily reflect the views or policies of the Service, nor does mention of trade names or commercial products constitute endorsement or recommendation for use. It is, however, exempt from review and compliance with MMS editorial standards.

REPORT AVAILABILITY

Extra copies of this report may be obtained from the Public Information Office (MS 5034) at the following address:

U.S. Department of the Interior
Minerals Management Service
Gulf of Mexico OCS Region
Public Information Office (MS 5034)
1201 Elmwood Park Boulevard
New Orleans, Louisiana 70123-2394

Telephone Number: (504) 736-2519 or
1-800-200 GULF

CITATION

Suggested citation:

Walker, N.D., E. Jarosz and S. P. Murray. 2001. An investigation of pressure and pressure gradients along the Louisiana/Texas inner shelf and their relationships to wind forcing and current variability. OCS Study MMS 2001-057. U.S. Dept. of the Interior, Minerals Management Service, Gulf of Mexico OCS Region, New Orleans, LA, 40 pp.

TABLE OF CONTENTS

LIST OF FIGURES

LIST OF TABLES

I. INTRODUCTION

The northwestern rim of the Gulf of Mexico is characterized by a broad, shallow shelf dominated by North American continental drainage, including the Mississippi and Atchafalaya Rivers and an array of smaller rivers and bays (Figure 1). The Mississippi/Atchafalaya River outflow produces buoyant, turbid plumes along the Louisiana coastline. This river system typically has a peak discharge during spring in excess of 30,000 m^3/sec and a low in autumn of about 10,000 m^3/s (Murray et al., 1998). The annual average discharge of the two rivers is 18,400 m^3/s (Milliman and Meade, 1983). A portion of the Mississippi River outflow, flowing westward, joins with the Atchafalaya River discharge forming a coastal current, termed the Louisiana Coastal Current (LCC) (Wiseman and Kelly, 1994). The latest studies (Murray et al., 1998) show that this current can be generally traced west of the Mississippi River delta along the entire Louisiana and Texas coasts. This current exhibits intense spatial and temporal variability related to the volume of river discharge and nature of the wind forcing (Murray et al., 1998).

Although circulation over the Louisiana/Texas shelf is complex and can vary rapidly, certain general circulation patterns have emerged from previous studies. On the inner shelf west of Atchafalaya Bay, surface circulation is primarily wind-driven and coherence has been found between alongshore wind-stress and alongshore currents for coastal locations (Smith, 1978; Crout et al., 1984; Lewis and Reid, 1985; Cochrane and Kelly, 1986; Murray et al., 1998). The wind-current relationship results in downcoast flow (westward/southward) along the Louisiana/Texas coast for much of the year with a coastal-type jet on the inner shelf (Cochrane and Kelly, 1986; Murray et al, 1998). The predominant east to west flow on the inner shelf is enhanced by the Atchafalaya and Mississippi River discharges. Short-lived flow reversals occur when winds blow from the west, as occurs with the passage of winter storms with recurrence frequencies of 3-10 days (DiMego et al., 1976). Longer-lived flow reversals occur during summer when strong southerly winds prevail along the south Texas coast and weak southerly and southwesterly winds blow along the Louisiana coast (Crout et al., 1984; Cochrane and Kelly, 1986; Jarosz et al., 1996; Murray et al., 1998; Walker and Hammack, 2000).

In this study, six pressure gauges were installed along the Louisiana/Texas inner shelf to enable a detailed investigation of the alongshore pressure and pressure gradients and their relationships to wind forcing and coastal circulation along the Louisiana/Texas coast. Lessons learned from observations, in the LCC (Murray et al., 1998) and other studies discussed above, suggest that alongshore variation in the pressure (water level) and pressure gradients may be of great importance in understanding the mechanisms controlling the Louisiana/Texas coastal current.

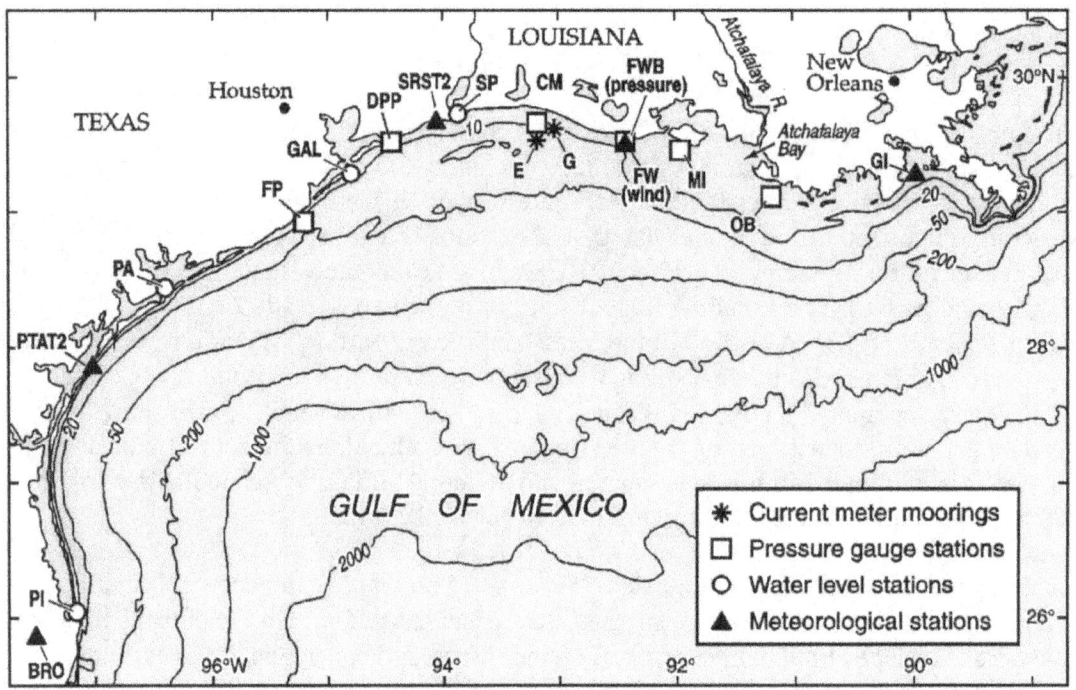

Figure 1. Map of the Louisiana/Texas (LATEX) continental shelf depicting the locations of pressure gauge, water level, meteorological and current meter measurements used in the study.

The primary objectives of this study were:

1. To deploy an alongshore near coastal pressure gauge array in order to understand the role of sea level slopes in the dynamics controlling the Louisiana Coastal Current.

2. To quantify the relationships between coastal wind stress and (1) sub-surface pressure (water level) and (2) alongshore pressure gradients.

3. To obtain a better understanding of the role of alongshore pressure gradients in coastal circulation changes.

4. To produce a data set of near coastal sea level and sea level slopes suitable for calibration and validation of numerical models of the Louisiana/Texas coastal current.

II. DATA AND METHODS

To analyze the sub-tidal temporal and spatial variability of sub-surface pressure and pressure gradients along the Louisiana-Texas coastline, six sub-surface pressure gauges were deployed in very shallow water (< 20m). These gauges were either SD 635 or SBE Seagauge instruments and they were set to record data with a 15-minute sampling interval. Most of the instruments were attached to existing offshore oil and gas platforms. The station called 'Dirty Pelican Pier' was attached to a piling leg of a pier. The locations of all gauges are listed in Table 1 and plotted in Figure 1.

Table 1
Locations and Abbreviations of Sub-Surface Pressure Gauge Stations, Water Level Stations and Meteorological Stations

Station Type	Station Name (abbreviation)	N. Latitude (degrees)	W. Longitude (degrees)
Pressure gauge	Oyster Bayou (OB)	29.12	91.18
Pressure gauge	Marsh Island (MI)	29.46	91.96
Pressure gauge	Freshwater Bayou (FWB)	29.53	92.42
Pressure gauge	Cameron (CM)	29.66	93.16
Pressure gauge	Dirty Pelican Pier (DPP)	29.52	94.46
Pressure gauge	Freeport (FP)	28.93	95.20
Water level	Sabine Pass, ID16 (SP)	29.73	93.87
Water level	Galveston Pleasure Pier, ID 509 (GAL)	29.29	94.79
Water level	Port O'Connor, ID 57 (PA)	28.45	96.41
Water level	Padre Island Coast Guard Station, ID 51 (PI)	26.07	97.17
Meteorological	GDIL1 (GI)	29.27	89.96
Meteorological	Freshwater Bayou (FW)	29.53	92.42
Meteorological	SRST2 (SP2)	29.67	94.05
Meteorological	PTAT2 (PA2)	27.83	97.05
Meteorological	Brownsville (BRO)	25.91	97.5

The gauges became operational in July 1994 and were kept in the specified locations until August 1995. Inspection of the recorded pressure time-series from this initial deployment revealed several periods of time with questionable or bad data that occurred mostly as a result of instrument malfunction. Faulty instrumentation was repaired and, for the most part, the sub-surface pressure gauges were returned to the same locations. The gauge at Dirty Pelican Pier was not re-deployed. The second recording period began in May 1996 and lasted through January 1998. The data inventory for both deployments (only periods with good data) are shown in Figure 2.

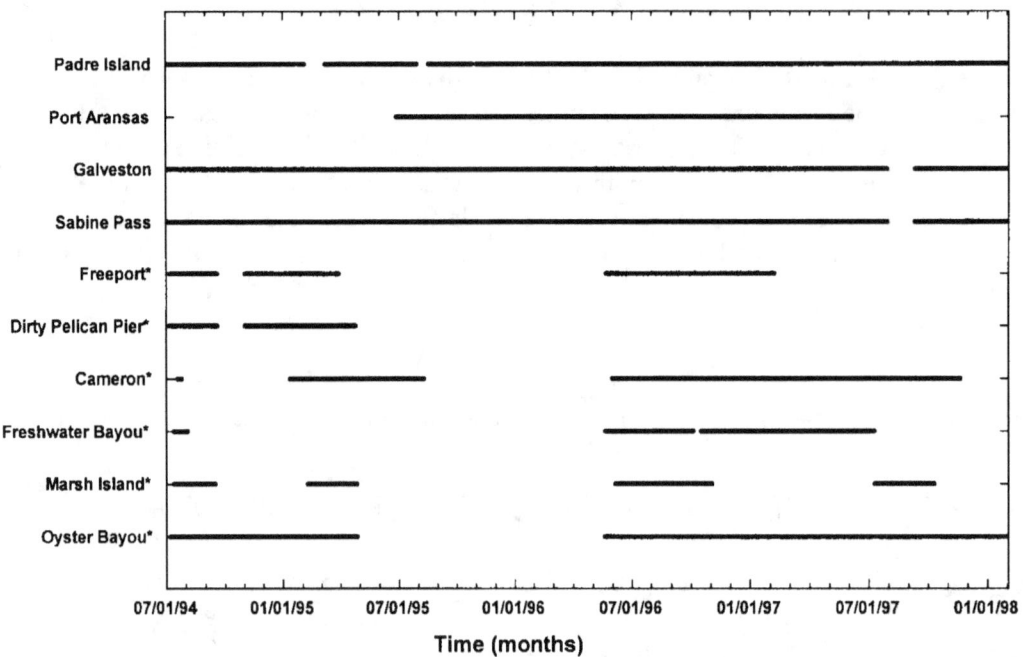

Figure 2. Inventory of sub-surface pressure gauge data (last six stations) collected in this study and additional coastal water level measurements (first four stations).

To improve the spatial coverage of the pressure and pressure gradient changes along the Louisiana-Texas coast, we also included four water level stations from the Texas coast in our analyses (see Table 1 and Figure 1 for their locations). Additional coastal measurements for Louisiana were not used as they were not representative of the coastal ocean due to placement in small channels. Prior to the analyses, the water level data was converted to sub-surface pressure and the atmospheric pressure was added to the time-series to make them comparable to the measurements acquired from our pressure gauges. The atmospheric pressure data used in these calculations were obtained from nearby CMAN stations.

Hourly wind measurements from the same CMAN stations, an airport at Brownsville, and an anemometer at Freshwater Bayou (see Table 1 and Figure 1 for their locations) were also analyzed together with the sub-surface pressure time-series to investigate pressure and pressure gradient responses to wind stress components.

The alongshore (u) and cross-shore (v) wind stress components were computed using the bulk aerodynamic equation with the drag coefficient (C_D) described by Large and Pond (1981), and used extensively in coastal and shelf dynamics studies (Brown et al., 1985; Brown and Irish, 1987; Lentz, 1995).

$C_D = 1.2 * 10^{-3}$ when $U_{10} < 11$ m/s
$C_D = (0.49 + 0.065U_{10}) * 10^{-3}$ when $U_{10} \geq 11$ m/s

4

In Hsu's (1988) review of drag coefficients, it can be seen that researchers have found a range of coefficients that vary by up to 30-40% over the range of wind speeds encountered in this study (0-15 m/s). Those of Large and Pond (1981) were on the low side of the drag coefficients reviewed by Hsu (1988). In this study, the statistical analyses (coherence squared) were normalized and thus not affected by the magnitude of the wind stress. Therefore, the use of a larger coefficient would not have altered the statistical results or conclusions resulting from them. Wind stress (N/m^2 was computed as

$$Tau_u = C_D * P * u \text{ component} * U_{10}$$
$$Tau_v = C_D * P * v \text{ component} * U_{10}$$

where P is the density of air and U_{10} is the wind speed in m/s at 10 m.

The alongshore and cross-shore components of the wind stress were fine tuned by rotating the original axes. The rotation angle depended on the location of the pressure gauge or, in the case of the pressure gradients, it depended on the location of a point midway between two gauges. All rotation angles are listed in Table 2 and are measured counterclockwise from east. Current meter measurements overlapping in time with the sub-surface pressure measurements were analyzed. These data were obtained for a different MMS project (Murray et al., in preparation) at moorings located on the shelf west of Atchafalaya Bay (Figure 1). Prior to the analyses, the sub-surface pressure data were averaged and hourly time series were generated. Then, for the majority of our analyses the hourly data were de-meaned and low-pass filtered to remove all fluctuations with periods less than 40 hours. To investigate time series variability and interdependence, the following statistical analyses were employed: spectra estimation, multiple, partial and ordinary coherence based on procedures described in Bendat and Piersol (1986). In addition to the wind stress, one may expect that sub-surface pressures may be influenced by freshwater discharge. To test this hypothesis, we also investigated whether Atchafalaya River discharge measured at Simmesport, LA caused any visible impact on sub-surface pressure fluctuations. Simmesport is located on the Atchafalaya River approximately 180 km north-northwest of Atchafalaya Bay (not shown).

Table 2
Rotation Angles for the Wind Stress Components

	Angle (degrees)
OB	335
MI	Station
FWB	350
CM	0
SP	19
DPP	25
GAL	25
FP	33
PA	55
PI	90

III. RESULTS AND DISCUSSION

A. The Annual and Semi-annual Cycles of Sub-surface Pressure/Water Level

The sub-surface pressure data and water level data worthy of investigation are depicted in Figure 2. Data collection began in July 1994 and ended in January 1998. Data retrieval was best between July 1996 and November 1997. For this reason, detailed analyses focused primarily on the latter time frame.

Figure 3 depicts the monthly averaged pressure/water level measurements for the entire data collection period. The available measurements indicate that coastal water levels usually reach their highest levels of the year during October. This was particularly evident in the Galveston and Sabine Pass records, that were most complete. October maxima were observed in available pressure measurements in each year from 1994 through 1997. The data indicate that the autumn maxima is usually larger in magnitude along the Texas coast. The data also indicate a secondary maxima in April/May of several years. The contemporaneous wind data show maximum westward alongshore wind stress in October and April/May of each year, corresponding with the water level maxima. There is a seasonal difference in the westward wind stress along the Louisiana coast. The strong westward wind stress in October has primarily a southward component, whereas the spring wind stress has primarily a northward component. This distinct seasonal change was also noted by Walker and Hammack (2000).

The water level/pressure minima were observed most often in January/February with secondary minima in July/June. These time periods corresponded with reductions in westward wind stress and increased eastward wind stress. The lowest water levels in winter are attributable to strong eastward and southward wind stress, forced by winter storms. The low water levels in summer may have resulted from a more sustained prevalence of northward wind stress along the Texas coast and eastward wind stress along the Louisiana coast. River discharge did not have a noticeable impact on the barotropic pressure or water level on the monthly time-scale. The highest river discharge within the time period of investigation occurred in April 1997, and there was no significant change in the monthly-averaged pressure even at stations closest to river influence, such as Oyster Bayou and Marsh Island. The range in monthly mean water levels over the year were as much as 40-45 mb (cm) along the Texas coast and 25-30 mb (cm) at Oyster Bayou (Figure 3). The use of sub-tidal data in the analysis would have reduced the coastal water level range by about 50% (Marmorino, 1982). Thus, the actual range in pressures over the semi-annual cycle were on the order of 80 to 90 cm. The annual cycle of atmospheric pressure is shown in Figure 4. It exhibits a fairly regular cycle with highest atmospheric pressure in winter (November-February) and lowest pressure from spring through summer. The annual range in monthly-averaged pressure was 6-8 mb. Thus atmospheric pressure can not explain the semi-annual cycle in coastal water levels due to the mismatch in timing as well as the much smaller magnitude in seasonal change. The available data indicate that changes in the direction and magnitude of wind forcing was the primary forcing agent for the semi-annual cycle in coastal water levels.

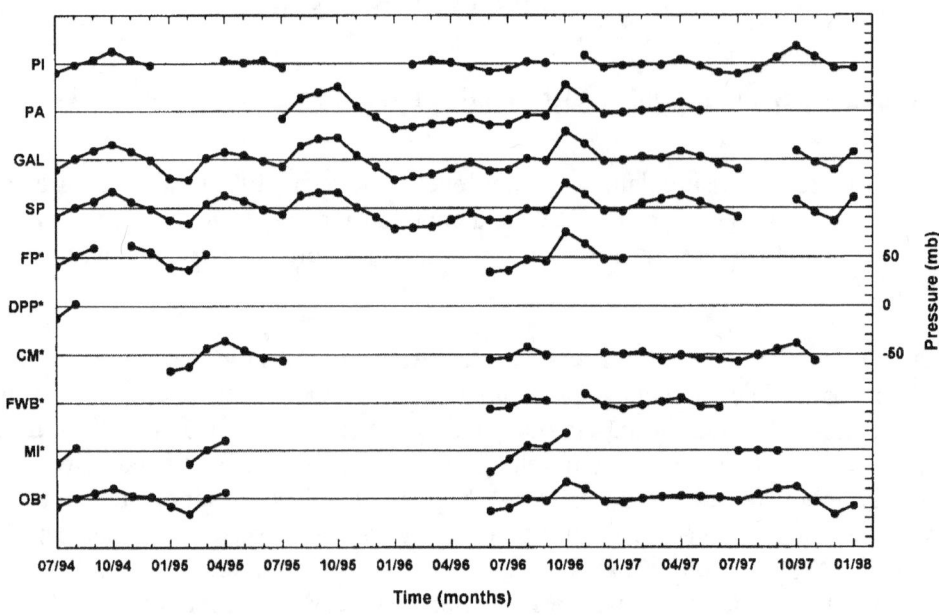

Figure 3. Monthly mean pressure measurements (de-meaned, 40 hour filtered) for all stations. The water level data were converted to sub-surface pressure and the sea level barometric pressure was added for consistency with the pressure gauge data. Asterisks denote pressure gauge stations.

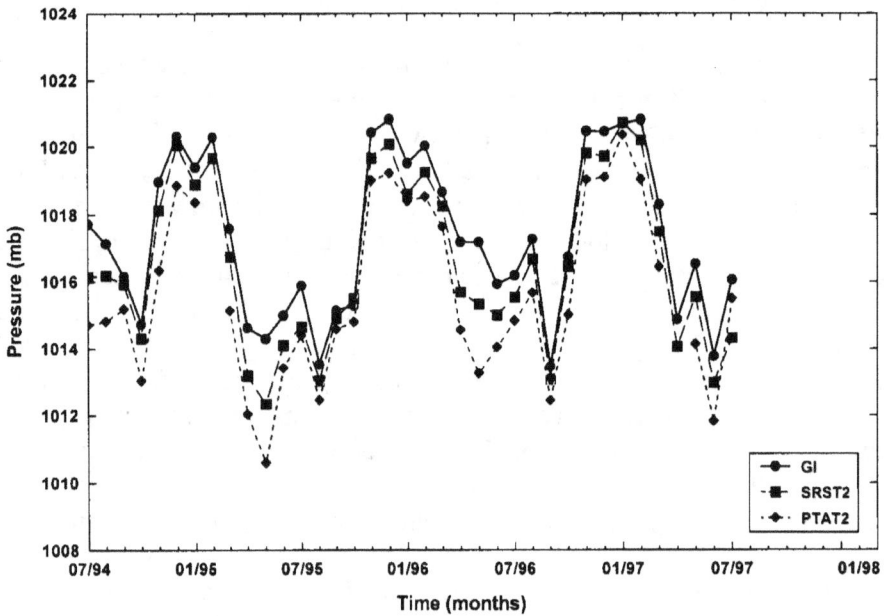

Figure 4. Monthly mean atmospheric pressure at three stations, GDIL1, SRST2 and PTAT2, in the study region

Similar timing of minima and maxima in coastal waters levels have been discussed previously by Whitaker (1971) and Sturges and Blaha (1976). Whitaker (1971) observed a large annual thermally-induced range in water level (about 13 cm) along the shelf break off Texas. The signal was characterized by a single minimum close in time to the vernal equinox and a single maximum near the autumnal equinox. He also found that the coastal water level (from 61 years) at

Galveston was in striking contrast to that along the shelf break as it exhibited an autumn peak of 13.5 cm and a secondary peak in late spring of 5.2 cm. The spring peak was thought to correspond with the maximum in freshwater discharge of the Mississippi and Atchafalaya Rivers. The primary minimum of -10.5 cm was in January with a secondary minimum of -4.4 cm in July. These values were adjusted for atmospheric pressure variations. Current (1996) suggested that the coastal tidal records along the Texas-Louisiana shelf were due to the combination of thermally-induced, wind-induced and riverine-induced signals. Sturges and Blaha (1976) reported that the sea level minima occurred in July for all coastal tide stations around the Gulf of Mexico, a feature also discussed by Whitaker (1971). They attributed these minima to wind curl forcing. The abrupt increase in coastal water level between August and September was explained by the increase in wind stress, the peak in the seasonal cycle of stored heat and the rise of sea level that accompanies the relaxation of the summer wind (curl)-driven gyre.

The results of this study suggest that the primary forcing function for the semi-annual cycle in coastal waters levels in the Louisiana/Texas coastal regions is wind stress.

B. Wind Effects on Pressure/Water Level

The effects of wind stress on water level/pressure changes were initially investigated by examining graphical outputs of the alongshore and cross-shore wind stresses in tandem with the pressure measurements. In Figure 5, the monthly mean alongshore wind stress is compared with the pressure measurements. The stations of Oyster Bayou (Figure 5a) and Galveston (Figure 5b) were chosen to represent the coastal region. The graphs revealed a negative correlation between these variables. Correlations of -0.66 and -0.5 were obtained for the two stations, respectively. The negative correlations indicate a correspondence between downcoast (upcoast) wind stress and higher (lower) pressure along the coast. Downcoast refers to westward flow along the LA coast and southward flow along the TX coast. These relationships were investigated in more detail on shorter time-scales.

Two time periods were chosen for analysis based on data availability: February-April 1995 and August-October 1996. These time periods were chosen as they were relatively data-rich and both exhibited large changes in water levels. The water levels for all stations are shown in Figure 6. In general, the pressure measurements were coherent across the study region. Most of the synoptic-scale highs and lows were observable at each station. The monthly means (Figure 3) were clearly dominated by a few synoptic events within the months. These synoptic events were further investigated by comparing pressures from selected stations with the alongshore and cross-shore wind stresses (Figures 7, 8). The Marsh Island and Galveston records were chosen to represent the study region. On the synoptic scale, highest water levels corresponded with downcoast-directed wind stress (westward/LA and southwestward/TX wind stress). Conversely, lowest water levels corresponded with upcoast-directed wind stress. Along the Louisiana coast, a large pressure change of about -80 mb (cm) occurred on 3/8/95 (Figure 7a) that corresponded with large changes in both alongshore and cross-shore wind stress. However, only the alongshore wind stress change could be dynamically related to the pressure change as it would have induced coastal water level set-down. This wind event did not produce a similar response along the Texas inner shelf, as the wind in that region was predominantly cross-shore. Along the Texas coast, the lowest pressure was recorded February 5 and the highest on March 30 (Figure 7b). Only the alongshore wind was

9

different during these contrasting events. The cross-shore stress was the same sign during both events, whereas the alongshore stress switched from positive stress of 0.04 N/m² in the 1st event to –0.07 N/m² during the 2nd (Figure 7b).

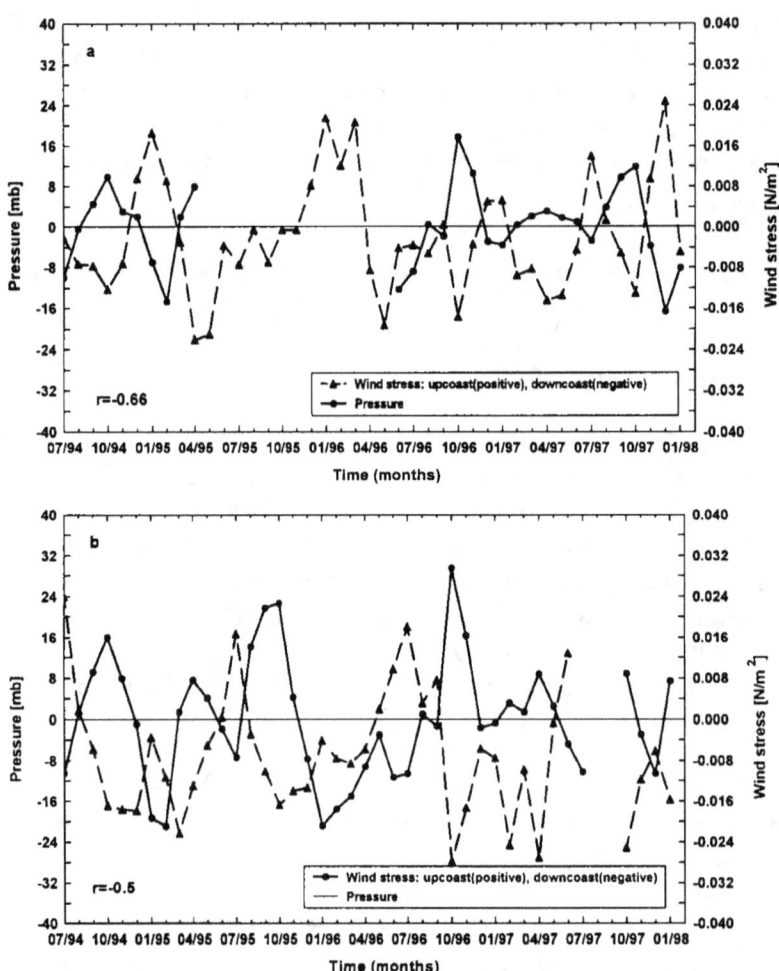

Figure 5. Monthly mean sub-surface pressure and alongshore components of pseudo wind stress for (a) Oyster Bayou pressure/Grand Isle wind and (b) Galveston pressure/SRST2 wind.

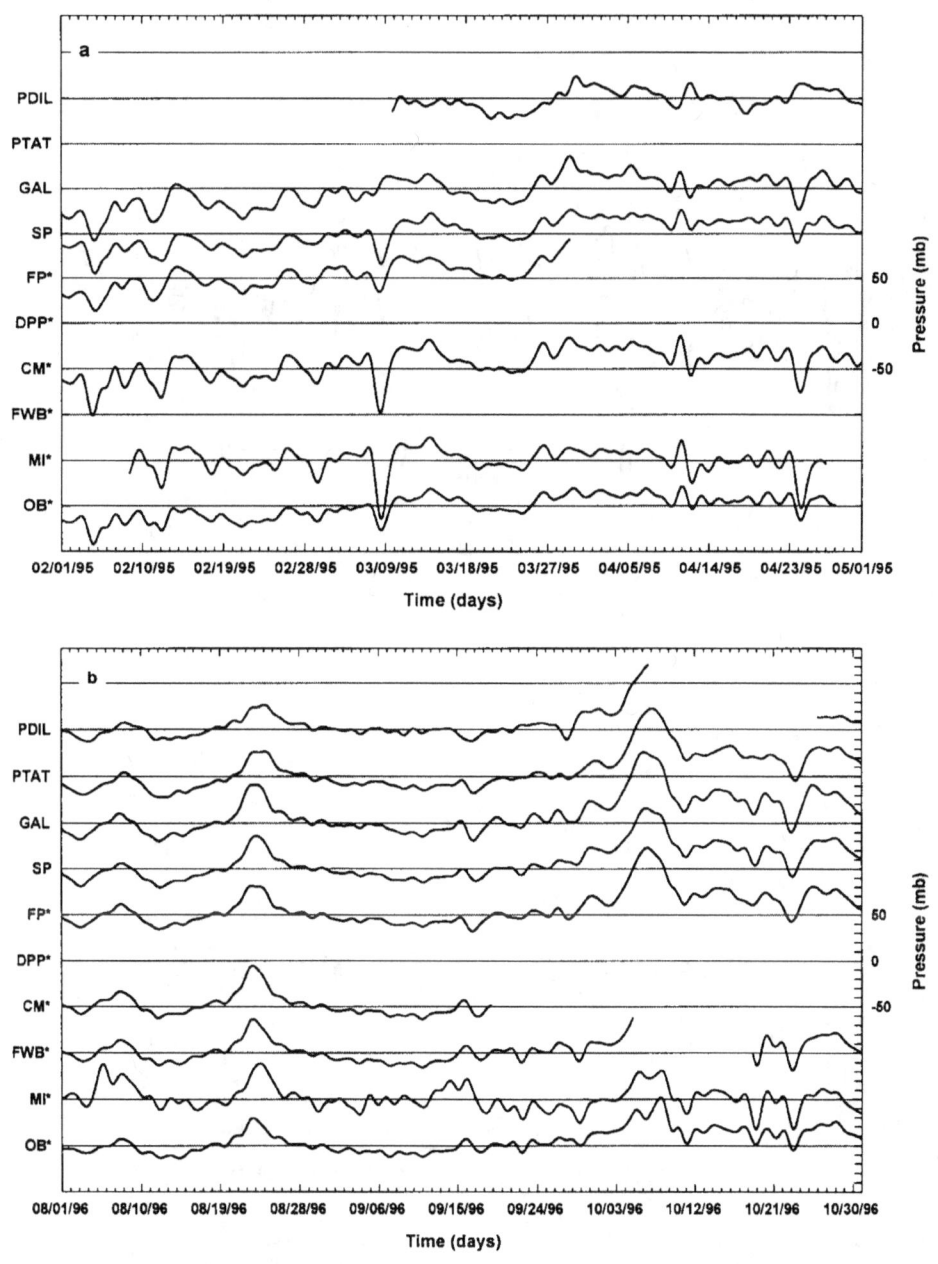

Figure 6. De-meaned and low-pass filtered pressure measurements at all stations for the time periods (a) February-April 1995 and (b) August-October 1996.

11

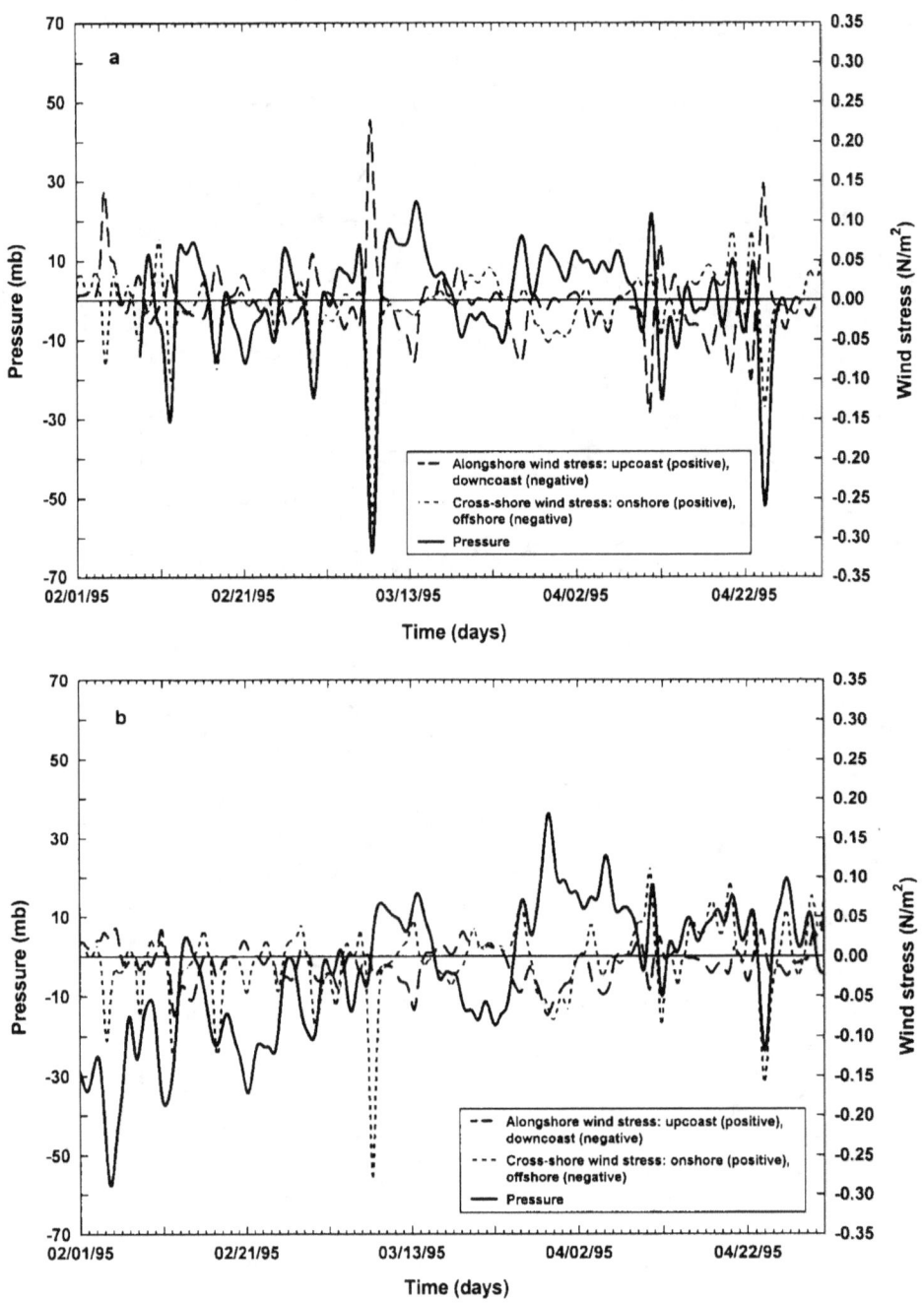

Figure 7. De-meaned and low-pass filtered pressure measurements, cross-shore and alongshore pseudo-wind stresses at (a) Marsh Island/Freshwater Bayou, LA and (b) Galveston/SRST2, TX during February-April 1995. Positive wind stress values represent upcoast alongshore flow and onshore cross-shore flow.

As a result of the change in orientation of the coastline across the study region, the relative magnitudes of the alongshore and cross-shore winds change. Along the eastern and central portion of the LA coast, the alongshore and cross-shore components were similar in magnitude and relatively strong. At FWB, maximum stresses in the alongshore direction were 0.23 N/m^2 and in the cross-shore direction were -0.32 N/m^2. The wind stress at SRST2 was less intense. At SRST2 there was more energy in the cross-shore than the alongshore direction. However, the pressure fluctuations were better correlated with the alongshore wind stress changes.

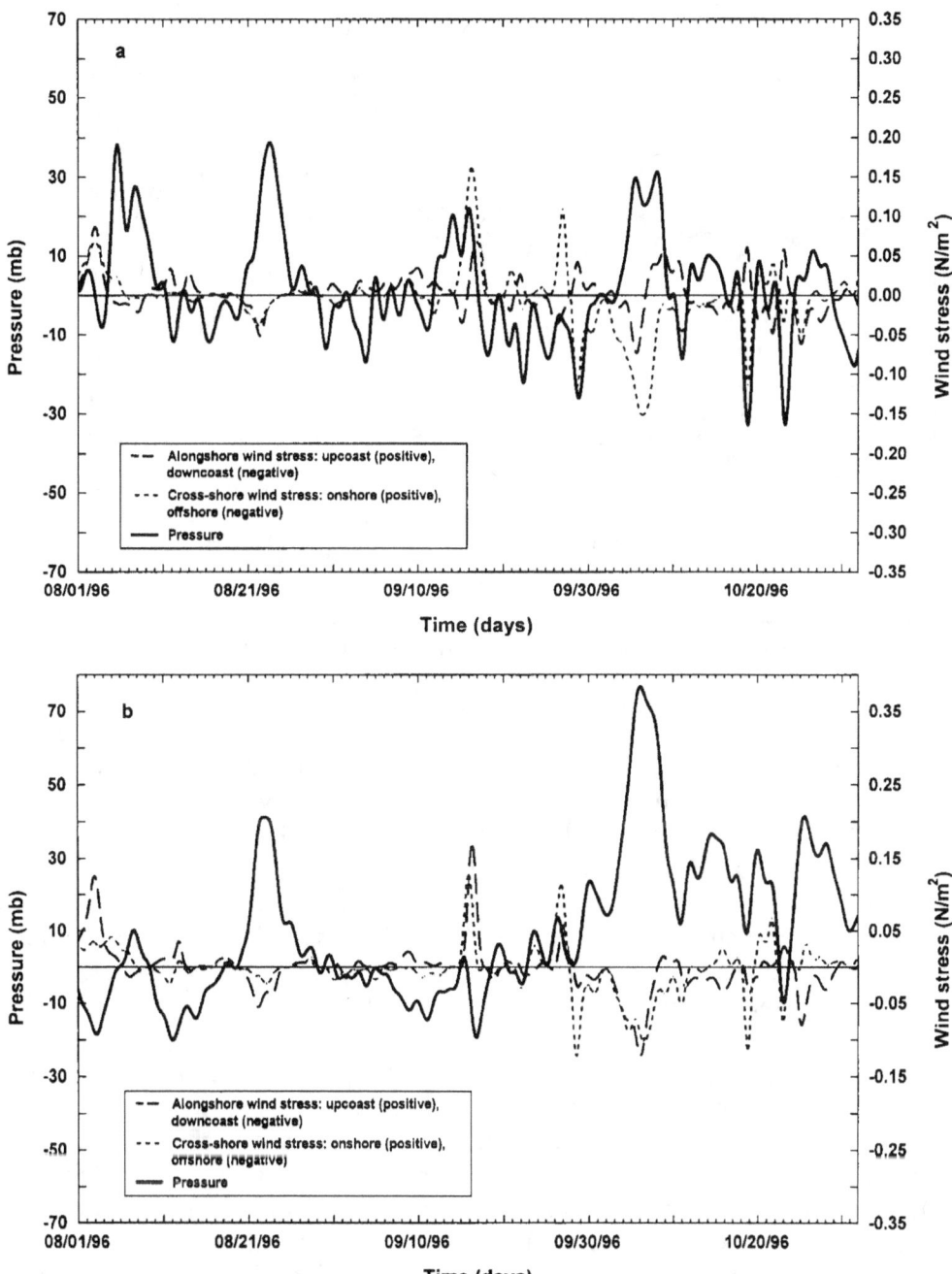

Figure 8. De-meaned and low-pass filtered pressure measurements, cross-shore and alongshore wind stresses at (a) Marsh Island/Freshwater Bayou, LA, (b) Galveston/SRST2, and (c) Oyster Bayou/Freshwater Bayou, LA during August-October 1996. Positive wind stress values represent upcoast alongshore flow and onshore cross-shore flow.

13

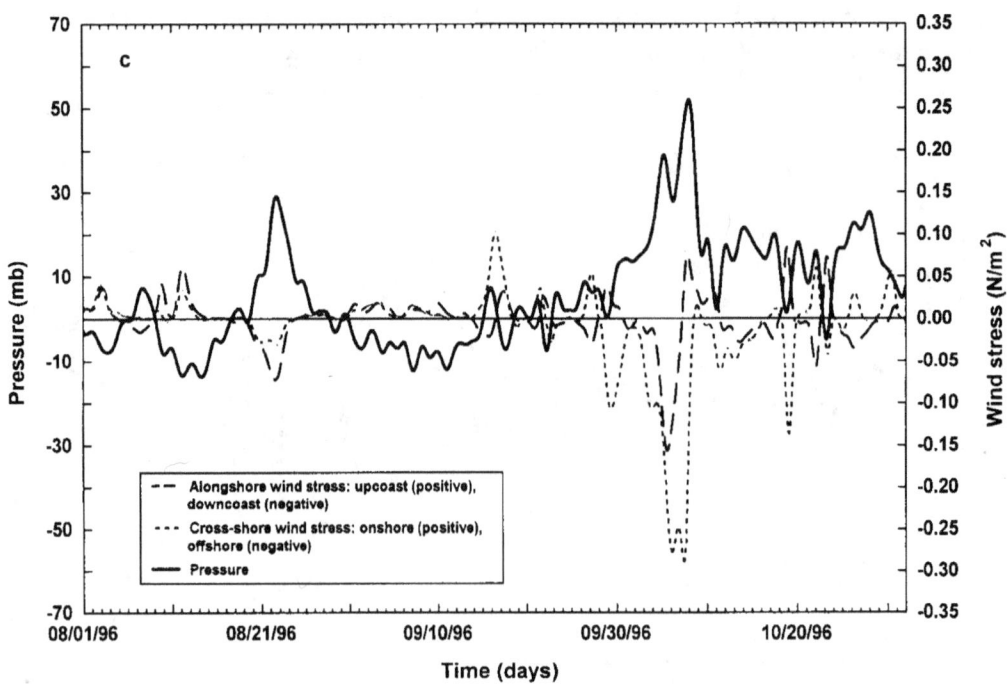

Figure 8 (continued). De-meaned and low-pass filtered pressure measurements, cross-shore and alongshore wind stresses at (a) Marsh Island/Freshwater Bayou, LA, (b) Galveston/SRST2, and (c) Oyster Bayou/Freshwater Bayou, LA during August-October 1996. Positive wind stress values represent upcoast alongshore flow and onshore cross-shore flow.

Analysis of pressures and wind during the second time period, August 1-October 31, 1996 revealed that the October pressure maxima resulted from one major event in early October (Figure 8a,b). Two distinct pressure maxima occurred at all stations within the study region, on 8/23/96 and 10/6/96. Both events were closely associated with distinct wind events. Along the LA coast, the water level maxima coincided with strong southwestward wind stress, however, the alongshore stress provided the major forcing mechanism for the water level rise. Southwestward winds also blew along the Texas coast, and with the change in coastal geometry, stronger alongshore stress occurred compared with the LA coast.

The strongest alongshore wind stress values of -13 N/m^2 occurred near Galveston (at SRST2) and a corresponding pressure increase of 120 mb occurred at the Galveston station between October 2 and 7 (Figure 8b). The Louisiana pressure change was about 60 mb during the same time period. The lowest pressure/water level occurred at different times along the coast. At PA and SP, the minima were experienced in August and coincided with strong winds from a southerly direction. August is the tail end of the summer upwelling season along the Texas coast (Walker, 2001). The lowest water levels at MI occurred in mid-October 1996 in concert with short-lived transitions to northwest winds (Figure 8a). The lowest water levels at OB occurred in August and September 1996 coincident with southwest winds (Figure 8c). These observations clearly indicate that the relative angle between the wind and the coastline are paramount in producing the pressure/water level response.

14

The close relationship between wind stress and coastal water levels is explained by Ekman transport processes (Csanady,1982). Sea levels are elevated to the right of the direction of the wind stress in the northern hemisphere. Thus, a wind blowing to the west along the LA coast would elevate water levels. Conversely, a wind blowing to the east along the LA coast would reduce water levels due to offshore transport of surface waters.

C. Spectral Analysis and Coherence of Pressure and Winds

Spectral analyses of the pressure measurements revealed peaks at the diurnal and semi-diurnal tidal frequencies at all stations. Where the time-series were relatively long, peaks were also revealed in the weather band frequency, between 2 and 10 days (Figure 9). The longest series of Freeport measurements revealed small weather band peaks at 5 and 8 days (Figure 9a). Measurements from Freshwater Bayou from October 1996 through July 1997 revealed two main peaks in the weather band (at 5 and 9 days) in addition to the tidal-related peaks (Figure 9b). The Oyster Bayou measurements revealed similar energy at the lower frequencies with five peaks between 2 and 20 days (not shown). In general, the results were not unexpected as they revealed the impacts of weather systems passing through the region between 5 and 9 days. Oyster Bayou exhibited more complexity than the other stations, perhaps due to the close proximity of two major rivers.

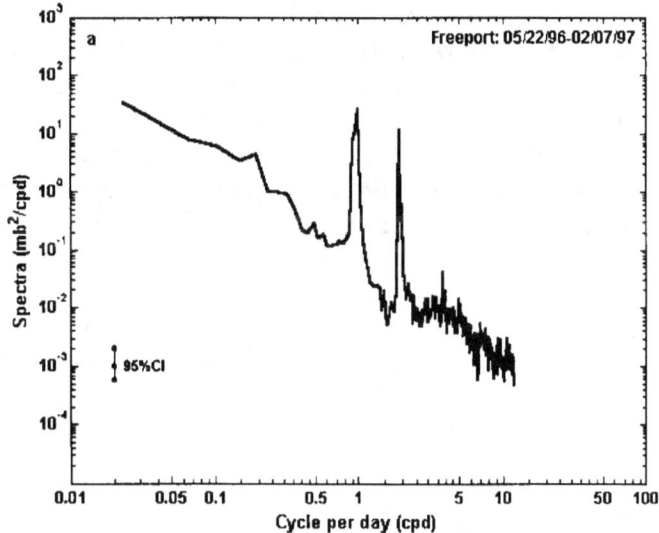

Figure 9. Spectra of pressure for (a) Freeport from May 22, 1996-February 7, 1997 and (b) Freshwater Bayou from October 20,1996-July 11, 1997.

15

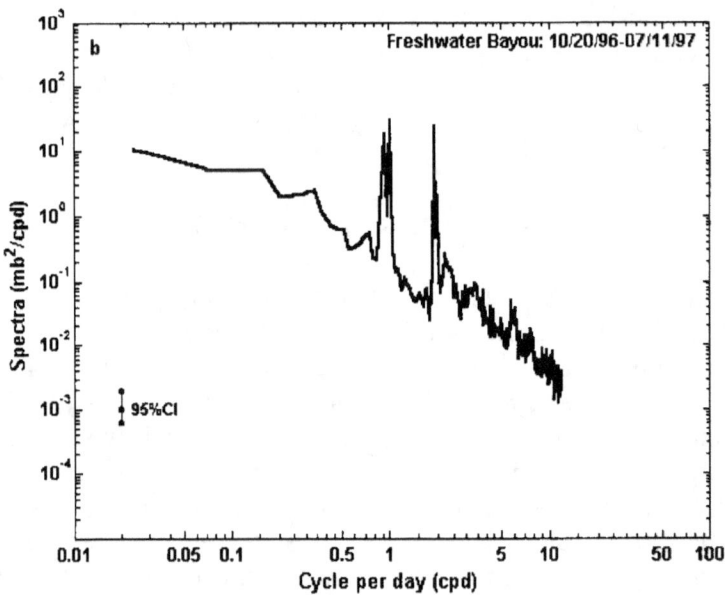

Figure 9 (continued). Spectra of pressure for (a) Freeport from May 22, 1996-February 7, 1997 and (b) Freshwater Bayou from October 20,1996-July 11, 1997.

One year of wind measurements from Freshwater Bayou was used to investigate the energy spectra of clockwise and counter-clockwise winds (Figure 10). The results revealed more energy in the counter-clockwise direction, which is the direction of rotation when pressure systems move from west to east across the study area. However, the clockwise-rotating winds also produced a peak, albeit less significant than the counter-clockwise wind peak. The largest weather-band peak was observed at 9-10 days. It is interesting that additional higher frequency peaks were observed corresponding to the diurnal period, perhaps indicating wind rotations associated with the coastal sea breeze-land-breeze system.

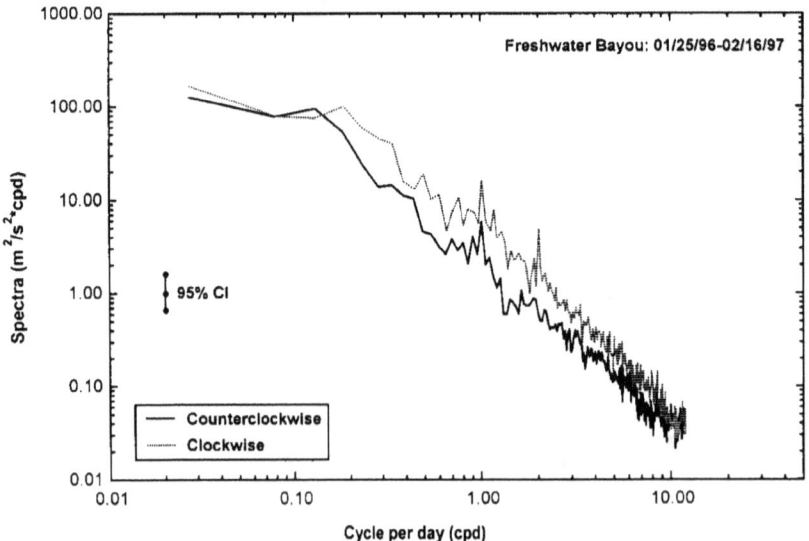

Figure 10. Spectra of counter-clockwise and clockwise rotating winds from Freshwater Bayou from January 25, 1996, through February 16, 1997.

Although the three spectra represented different time periods, the pressure and wind spectra both revealed repetitive events with a frequency of about 9 days. Albeit small, the peaks may have physical meaning in that this time period corresponds with the winter storm frequency. It is conceivable that the strongest winter storms with significant alongshore wind stress occur with such a frequency. Peaks were also observed in the pressure spectra at 5 days, a frequency that also falls in the range reported for winter storm frequency (DiMego et al., 1976).

The multiple and partial coherences between pressure and wind stress were estimated based on the spectral energy density information. Summer and winter periods were treated separately in order to enable the detection of possible seasonal differences in the relationships between pressure and wind. Tables 3 and 4 summarize the main results from the coherence analyses between pressure and the alongshore and cross-shore wind stresses by season. An attempt was made to use the same or similar summer and winter time periods for all stations. The summer period chosen was 6/1/96 to 8/31/1996. The winter period varied, however, most data were obtained between 9/1/96 and 5/31/97. The data from Cameron covered the period 1/11/95 to 5/31/95.

Table 3

The Highest Observed Partial Coherence Squared Values between <u>Pressure</u> and the <u>Alongshore Wind Stress</u> for Summer and Winter Periods. The Period in Days Is Rounded to Nearest Whole Number.

Station	Summer		Winter	
	Time period (days)	Partial Coherence	Time period (days)	Partial Coherence
OB	6-20	> 0.8	7-11	>0.7
MI	6	0.68	2-5	0.77
FWB	5-10	> 0.75	6-20	> 0.8
CM	13	0.62	7	0.65
SP	5-10	0.74	5	0.76
GAL	13	0.7	8	0.8
FP	5	0.48	5	0.8
PA	5	0.5	7	0.8
PI	5	0.5	3	0.68

Table 4

The Highest Observed Partial Coherence Squared Values between <u>Pressure</u> and the <u>Cross-Shore Wind Stress</u> for Summer and Winter Periods. Ns Indicates Non-Significance at the 95% Level. The Period in Days Is Rounded to Nearest Whole Number.

Station	Summer		Winter	
	Time period (days)	Partial Coherence	Time period (days)	Partial Coherence
OB		NS	4	>0.7
MI	3	0.5	3	0.6
FWB	3	0.43	2	> 0.7
CM	3	0.3	2	0.35
SP	6-7	0.6	2	0.76
GAL	5	0.45	3	0.72
FP	3	0.28	5	0.4
PA	5	0.5	7	0.55
PI	5	0.5	6	0.3

At all stations and in all seasons, the alongshore wind stress exhibited higher coherences with pressure changes than did the cross-shore wind stress. In the cases where the cross-shore wind stress did exhibit significant coherence with the pressure, it was often at a higher frequency. Along the LA coast, the partial coherences between pressure and alongshore wind stress ranged from 0.7-0.8. during both summer and winter, at frequencies between 2 and 20 days (Table 3). Graphs of the coherence results from OB and FWB are depicted in Figures 11 and 12. At both stations, coherences with the alongshore wind stress were higher than with the cross-shore stress. Coherences between pressure and cross-shore wind stress were higher during autumn and winter as compared with summer (Table 4). The cross-shore wind stress would be expected to increase in winter with the increase in frequency of winter storms and offshore winds, perhaps explaining this seasonal difference. At OB and FWB, the cross-shore wind stress explained as much as 70% of the variability in winter pressure (Figure 11) in the 2-4 day frequency range. This result corroborates the findings of Chuang and Wiseman (1986) as they also showed that the shallow Atchafalaya Bay water levels respond strongly to cross-shelf wind forcing.

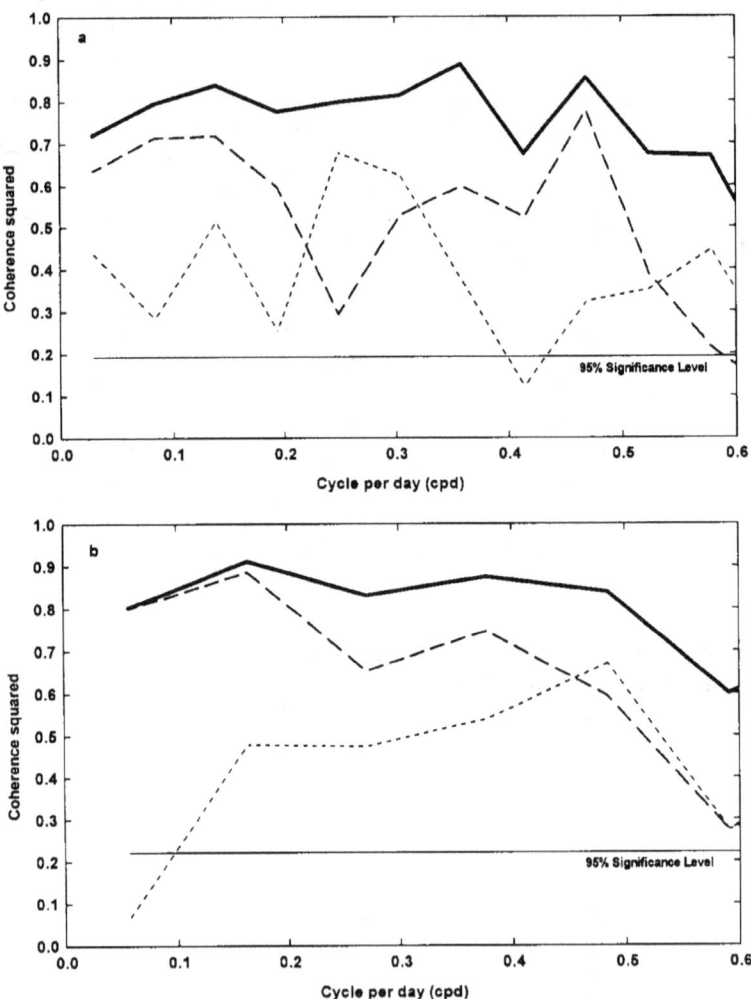

Figure 11. Multiple and partial coherence squared estimates between pressure and wind stress for an autumn/winter period at (a) Oyster Bayou (9/1/96-5/31/97) and at (b) Freshwater Bayou (10/17/96-2/16/97). The solid line depicts the multiple coherence. The partial coherence for alongshore wind stress is shown as a dashed line. The partial coherence for cross-shore wind stress is depicted with a dotted line.

18

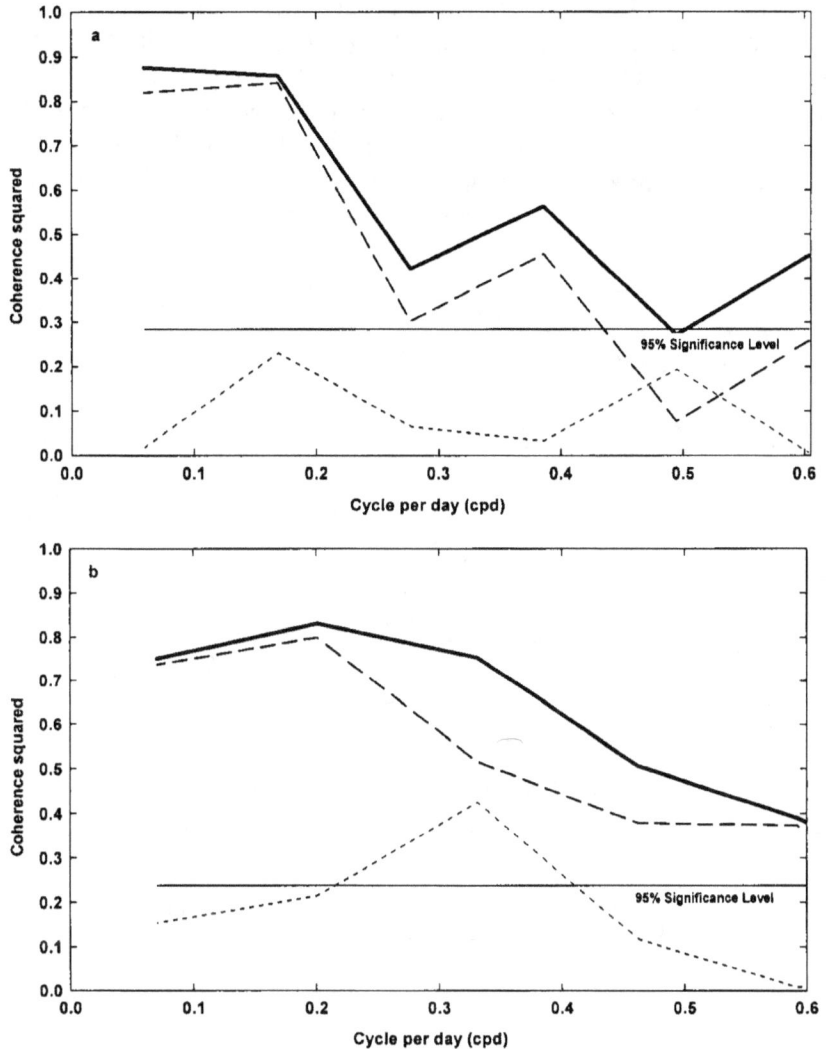

Figure 12. Multiple and partial coherence squared estimates between pressure and wind stress for a summer period at (a) Oyster Bayou (6/1/96-8/31/96) and at (b) Freshwater Bayou (6/1/96-8/31/96). The solid line depicts the multiple coherence. The partial coherence for alongshore wind stress is shown as a dashed line. The partial coherence for cross-shore wind stress is depicted with a dotted line.

The Cameron results stood out as unusual compared with those further to the east. At that site, the cross-shore wind stress was not coherent with the pressure during either the summer or winter seasons. The partial coherences between pressure and alongshore wind stress were 0.62-0.65 in both summer and winter in the time period of 7 to 13 days. The Sabine coherence results (not shown) were similar to those of Oyster Bayou and Freshwater Bayou, but slightly higher. The locations of the wind stations along the Louisiana and Texas coasts may have significantly influenced these results.

The Texas stations exhibited seasonal differences in the pressure/alongshore wind coherence results as the values were higher during winter than summer, especially south of Galveston (Table 3). A similar seasonal difference was noted at Galveston and Freeport in the cross-shelf coherence estimates (Table 4). During winter, highest coherences between pressure changes at Texas coastal stations and wind stress were 0.7-0.8 between 3 and 8 days. During summer, coherences were somewhat lower (0.48-0.7) between 5 and 13 days (Table 3). The greatest seasonal changes were observed at Freeport where coherences were as high as 0.8 in the winter, however, only 0.48 in the summer. (Figure 13). The Port Aransas and Padre Island results (not shown) were similar to those obtained for Freeport. Overall, the coherences between cross-shore wind stress and pressure at Texas stations during winter ranged from 0.3-0.72 between 3 and 8 days (Table 4).

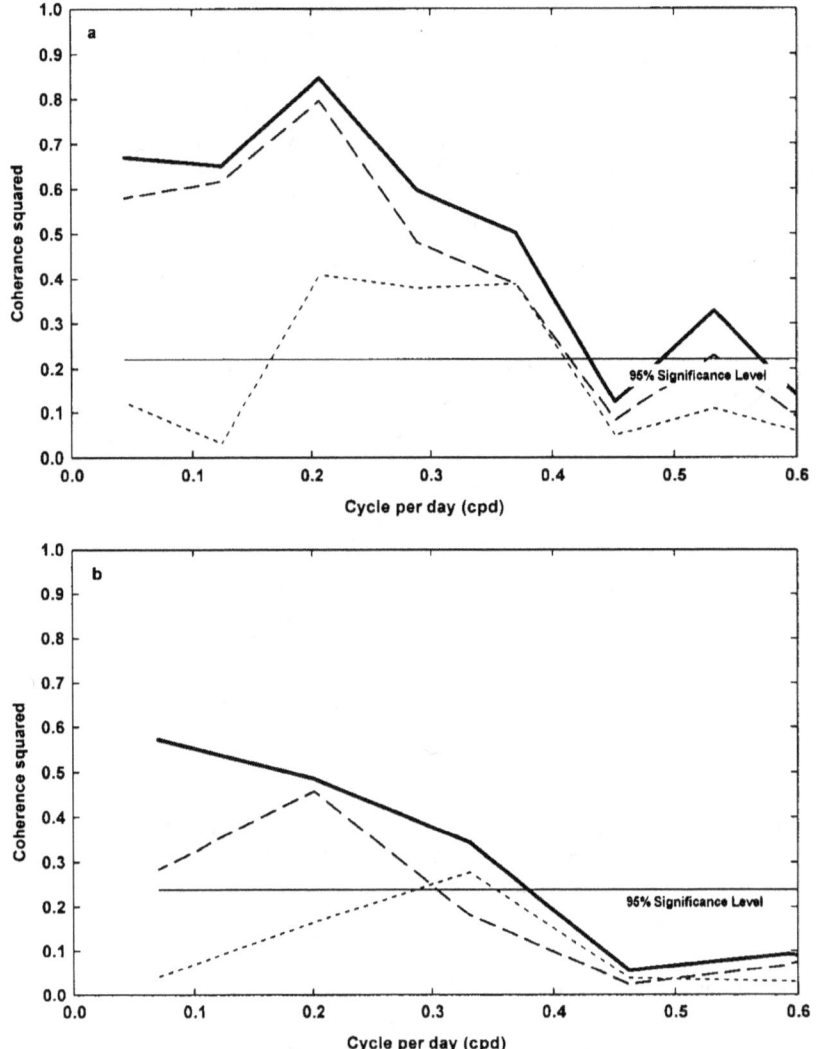

Figure 13. Multiple and partial coherence squared estimates between pressure and wind stress at Freeport, TX during (a) autumn/winter (9/1/96-2/7/97) and (b) summer (6/1/96-8/31/96). The solid line depicts the multiple coherence. The partial coherence for alongshore wind stress is shown as a dashed line. The partial coherence for cross-shore wind stress is depicted with a dotted line.

At some stations, more than one seasons' data were analyzed and considerable inter-annual variability in the coherence estimates were detected. For example, the relationships between pressure and wind stresses did not remain the same from summer to summer at Padre Island. The coherence estimates between pressure and alongshore wind stress were notably higher during the June-August 1997 time period (Figure 14b), compared with June-August 1996 (Figure 14a).

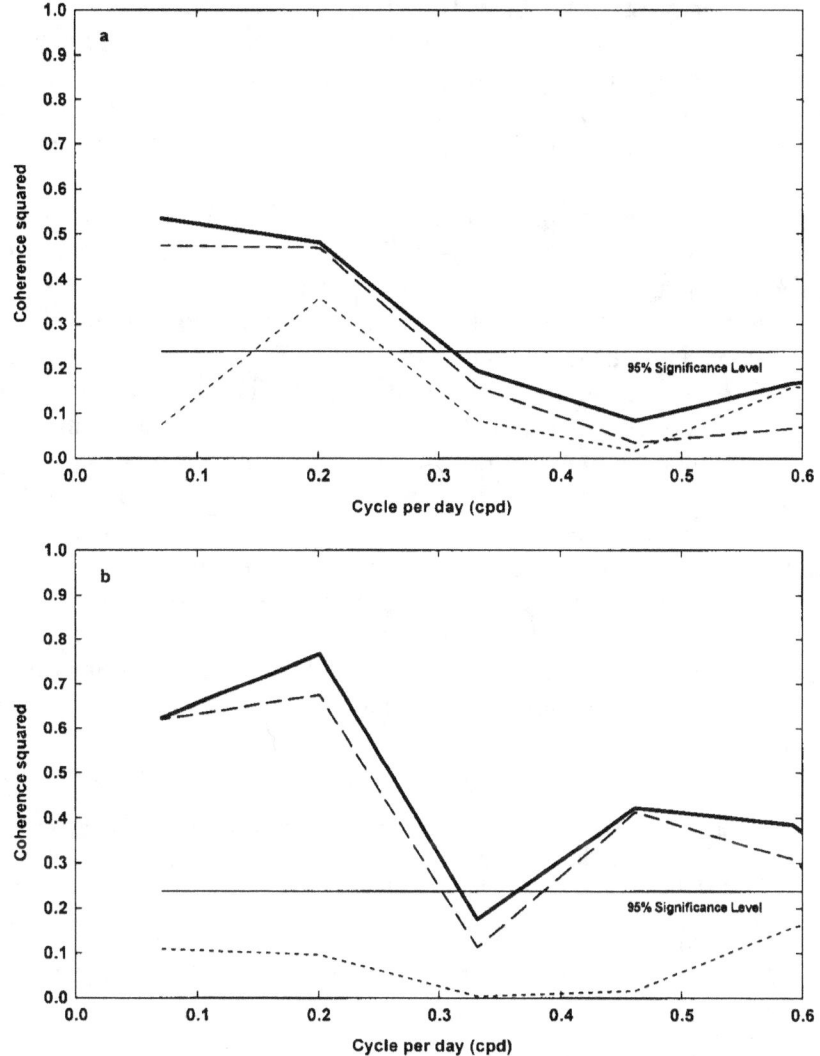

Figure 14. Multiple and partial coherence squared estimates between pressure and wind stress at Padre Island, TX during two summers (a) 6/1/96-8/31/96 and (b) 6/1/97-8/31/97. The solid line depicts the multiple coherence. The partial coherence for alongshore wind stress is shown as a dashed line. The partial coherence for cross-shore wind stress is depicted with a dotted line.

The results of this analysis demonstrated that the variability in coherence between wind and pressure is quite large along the Louisiana and Texas coastline. Some of the variations may be attributable to the lack of coastal wind stress data suitable for comparison with the pressure/water level data. The discharge from major rivers and estuarine regions may also contribute complexity and variability to the datasets.

D. Coherence Between Alongshore Pressure Gradients, Wind Forcing and Currents

The coherences between pressure gradients (difference between station pressures) and wind stress (alongshore and cross-shore) were investigated using all possible station combinations. Table 5 depicts the highest coherence estimates obtained between pressure gradients and the alongshore wind stress. Coherences were very low between the cross-shore wind stress and pressure gradients along this entire coastal region and, therefore, will not be shown or discussed.

Along the Louisiana coast, the strongest coherences were identified using alongshore pressure gradients and alongshore wind forcing between Oyster Bayou and all other stations. During the summer period, the maximum coherences were at periods of 7 and 20 days (Table 5). The highest coherences were obtained for Oyster Bayou and Freshwater Bayou in the 7-20 day period (coherences > 0.77), perhaps due to their close proximity. This result may be partially attributable to the influence of the Atchafalaya River plume that is discharged onto the shelf between these stations. The river effluent responds quickly to changes in wind forcing (Walker et al., 1997; Murray et al., 1998; Walker and Hammack, 2000) and its movements could augment pressure gradients along this part of the coast. The pressure gradient/wind coherences between Marsh Island and all other stations were relatively low (< 0.5) and at shorter periods (3-4 days). The pressure gradient/wind coherences between Freshwater Bayou and the other stations were not significant. The same situation was found for Cameron. High coherences between pressure gradients and wind stress were observed at all stations between Sabine Pass and Padre Island. Most station pairs yielded coherences above 0.7 at a period of about 7 days (Table 5). For Louisiana station pairs, the coherences between pressure gradients and wind stress were somewhat higher during winter than during summer.

Table 5

The Highest Observed Partial Coherence Squared Values Between Pressure Gradients and the Alongshore Wind Stress for Summer and Winter Periods. Nd Indicates the Absence of Data. Ns Indicates Non-Significance at the 95% Level. The Period in Days Is Rounded to Nearest Whole Number.

| Station | Summer | | Winter | |
	Time period (days)	Partial Coherence	Time period (days)	Partial Coherence
OB/MI	3	0.57	ND	ND
OB/FWB	7-20	0.77-0.80	7	0.89
OB/CM	7-20	0.62-0.75	7	> 0.88
OB/SP	7	0.63	7	0.87
OB/GL	7	0.65	7	0.82
OB/FP	20	0.55	7	0.77
SP/GL	3	0.33	ND	0.76
SPFP	7	0.55	NS	ND
SP/PA	7	0.7	57	NS
SP/PI	7-20	0.62-0.78	7	0.7
GL/FP	7	0.8	7	0.82
GL/PA	7	0.75	7	0.72
GL/PI	7	0.72	7	0.72
FP/PA	7	0.66	7	0.7
FP/PI	7	0.53	7	0.66
PA/PI	7-20	0.52-0.59	7	0.7

Coherences were lowest when using pressure gradients between Louisiana and Texas stations in summer. For example, the coherence estimates for the station pair OB/FP was 0.77 in winter and 0.55 in summer. The time period of the maximum coherence estimates changed from 7 days in winter to 20 days in summer. The coherence estimates were even lower for the station pair SP/GL where in winter the coherence was 0.76 and in summer it fell to 0.33.

Less seasonal variability in coherences was observed when using station pairs along the Texas coast. The coherences between pressure gradients and alongshore wind stress between GL/FP, GL/PA and GL/PI ranged between 0.72-0.82 during summer and winter periods (Table 5). The lowest coherences were identified for the station pairs FP/PI and PA/PI in summer. Coherences at these station pairs were higher during winter. The relatively low coherences in summer along the southern Texas coast may result from a lack in alongshore pressure gradients since this is an area of strong winds and coastal upwelling (Walker, 2001). Alternatively, higher coherences may have been obtained using the wind stress curl.

Current meter measurements on the inner shelf near Cameron (Locations, Figure 1) were available for the selected summer and winter periods of this study (Murray et al., in preparation). Data from inner shelf stations are shown in Figure 15 in relation to the alongshore wind stress and Cameron pressure. The winter measurements reveal a close relationship between the Cameron currents and the alongshore wind stress (Figure 15a). Along-shelf flow reversals corresponded closely in time with reversals in the alongshore wind stress. Lags of one day were not uncommon. It is interesting to note that flow reversals occurred every 7-10 days during this winter period, agreeing with the statistical analyses, presented earlier. Visual inspection of the summer graph (Figure 15b) reveals that many current reversals also occurred soon after wind reversals. During this summer period, three prominent downcoast flow events (currents > 20 cm/s) occurred on June 7, July 18 and August 22 (Figure 15b). The first event occurred with very weak alongshore wind forcing whereas the second two events were forced by stronger winds. The Mississippi/Atchafalaya River reached its peak discharge in early June 1996. At Simmesport, the annual maximum of 12,492 m^3/s occurred on June 9 and the relatively strong currents on June 7-8 may have partially resulted from buoyancy forcing rather than primarily from wind forcing. By July 9, Simmesport discharge had decreased to 6500 m^3/s.

Seven major upcoast flow events occurred off Cameron in the June-August 1996 time period that generally corresponded with wind shifts (Figure 15b). Upwelling favorable winds started to blow locally on June 6 and within 24 hours a current reversal occurred. The upcoast flow persisted despite the cessation of favorable wind forcing. An upcoast favorable wind began to blow on June 14, however, currents only switched direction to upcoast on June 21. Once this upcoast flow was established, it persisted again despite the cessation in wind forcing. During July and August 1996, the current and wind reversals occurred closer in time. These observations suggest that the currents near Cameron may be controlled by pressure gradient effects at least during portions of the summer period.

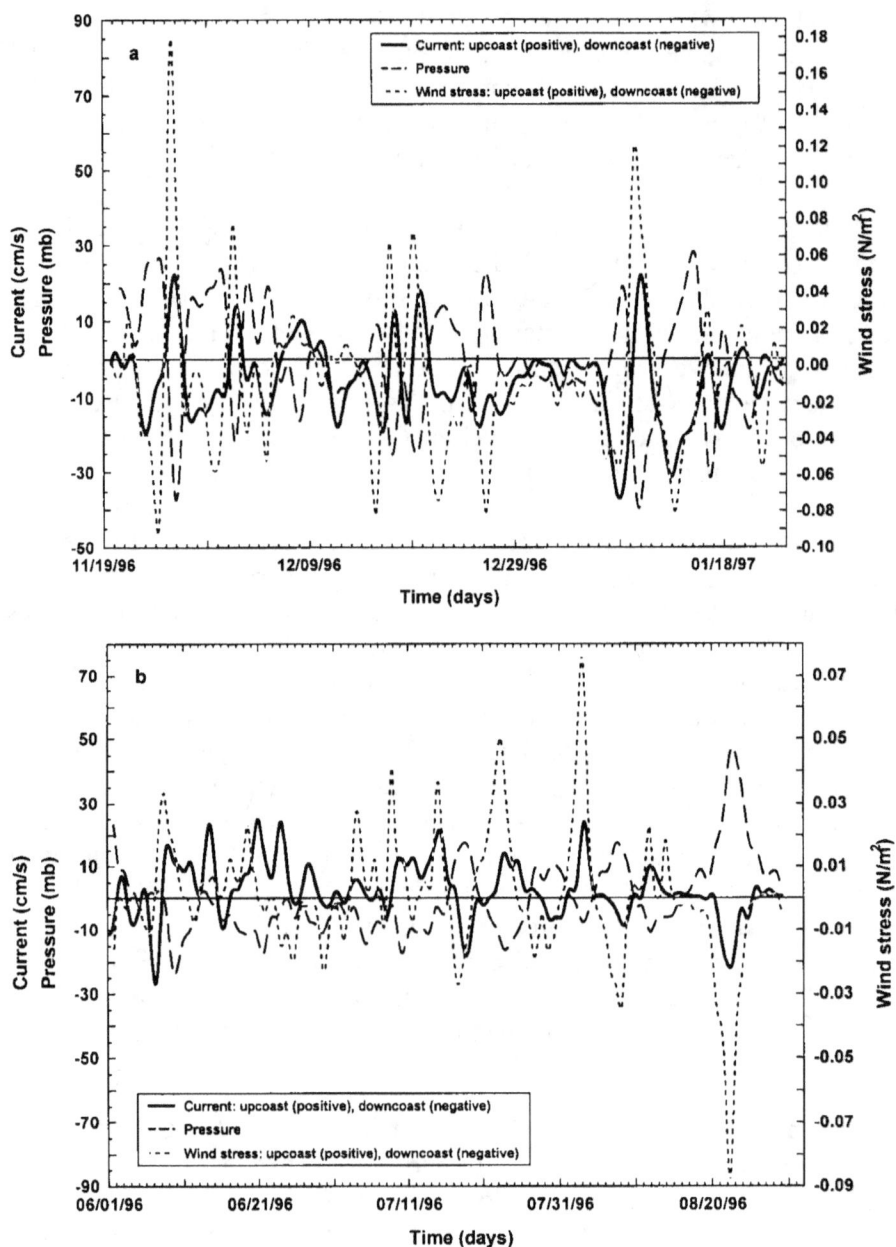

Figure 15. Near-surface inner shelf current meter measurements near Cameron, alongshore wind stress and Cameron sub-surface pressure for the time periods (a) 11/19/96-2/7/97 and (b) 6/1/96-8/31/96. Data from mooring G was available for the summer period and from mooring E for the winter time period. The current measurements are depicted with solid lines, the pressure with dashed lines and the alongshore wind stress with dotted lines.

A previous investigation compared currents off Cameron and pressure gradients between Oyster Bayou and Freeport (Murray et al., in preparation). In that study, the currents were found to oppose the pressure gradients between these two sites, indicating that the currents on the inner shelf near Cameron were not controlled by alongshore pressure gradients. These relationships were further investigated in this study. Close inspection of graphical outputs revealed correlations between the Cameron currents and the pressure gradients between Sabine Pass and Padre Island (Figure 16). The records were negatively correlated as the downcoast currents were experienced after the establishment of an upcoast pressure gradient. Seven events are indicated on Figure 16b. The development of strong negative pressure gradients (Sabine-Padre Island) can be visually correlated to the subsequent upcoast flow events at Cameron. This result led to the investigation of the statistical relationships between Cameron currents and pressure gradients between Padre Island and Sabine Pass.

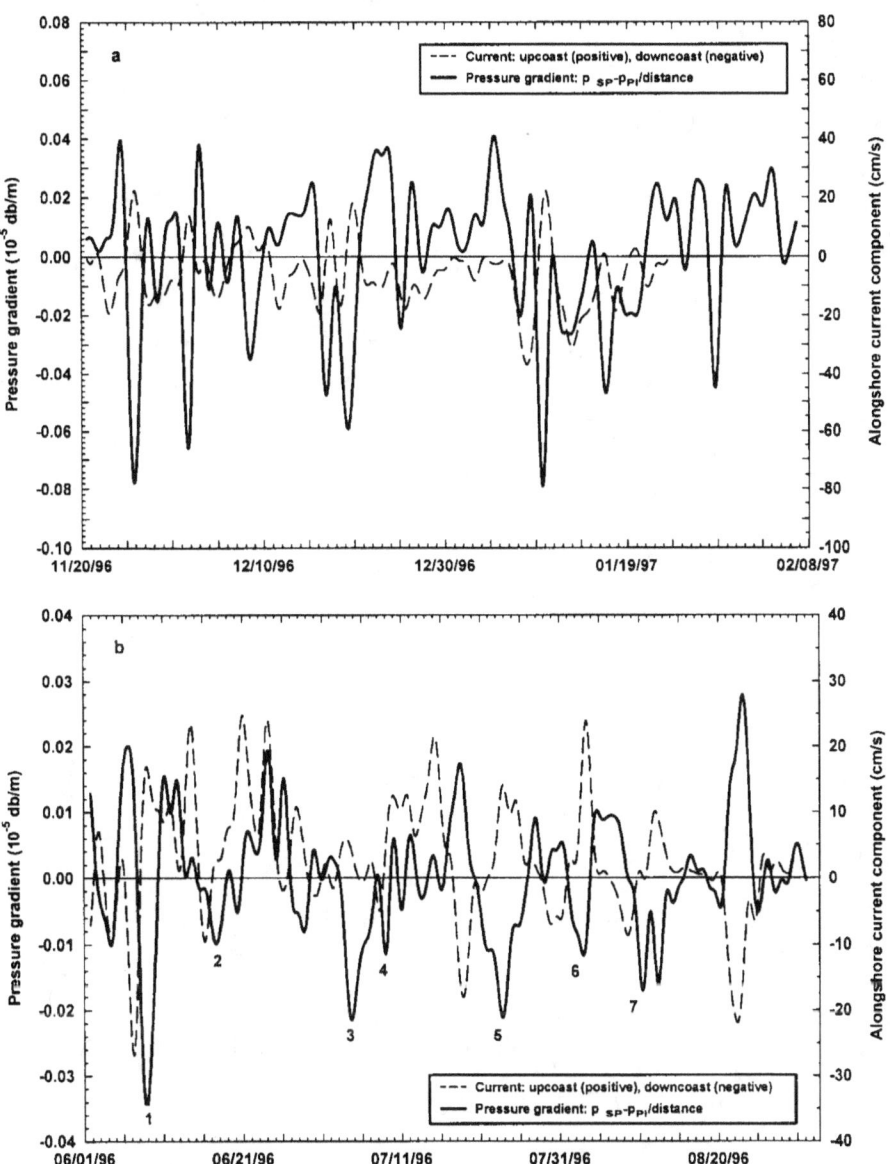

Figure 16. Near-surface inner shelf current meter measurements near Cameron compared with the Sabine Pass-Padre Island pressure gradient for the time periods (a) 11/20/96-2/7/97 and (b) 6/1/96-8/31/96. Up-coast flow events associated with pressure gradient events are noted in (b) with numbers 1-7. Data from mooring G were available for the summer period and from mooring E for the winter period. The current measurements are depicted with dashed lines and the pressure gradients with solid lines.

The analysis of coherence squared estimates between the alongshore current velocities at mooring G off Cameron (Figure 1 for location) and pressure gradients between Sabine Pass and Padre Island revealed a statistically significant relationship during the summer period, June 1 through August 31, 1996 (Figure 17b). Over 60% of the variability in currents was coherent with the pressure gradient in the period of 5-7 days. No significant relationship between inner shelf currents (mooring E) and pressure gradients were found in the winter period, October 25-January 24, 1997 (F

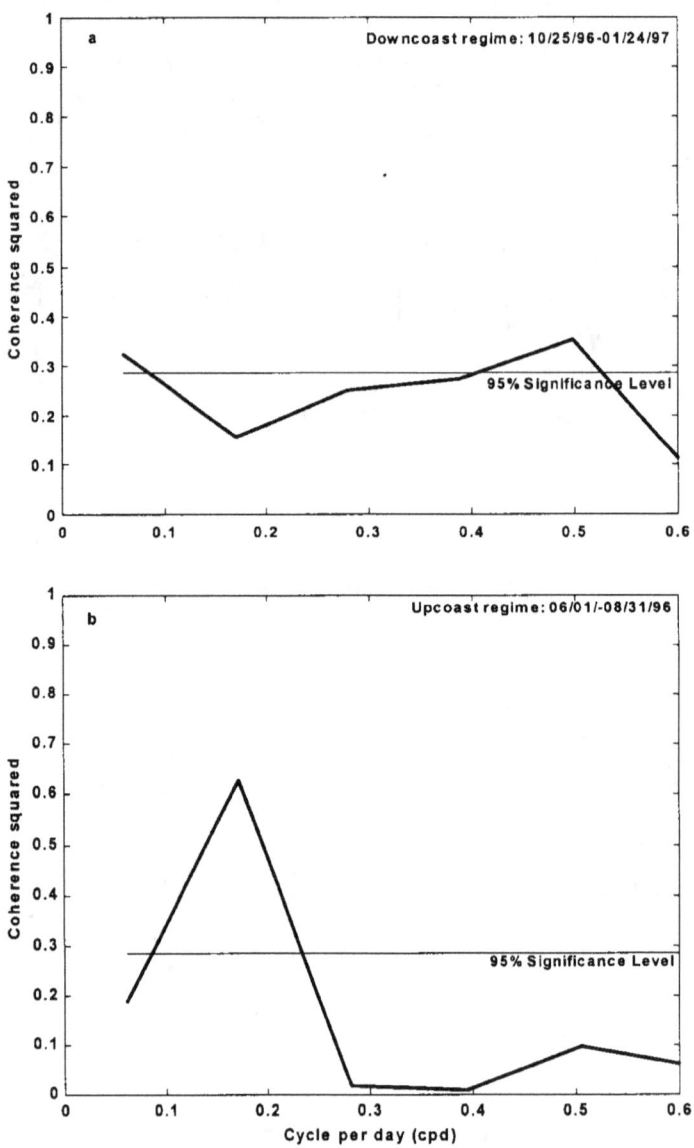

Figure 17. Coherence squared between current meter measurements on the inner shelf near Cameron and the pressure gradient between Sabine Pass and Padre Island from (a)10/25/96 to1/24/97 and (b) 6/1/96 to 8/31/96.

E. Winter Storm Forcing of Sub-Surface Pressure and Pressure Gradient Changes

On the synoptic time scale, a dominant meteorological disturbance in the northern Gulf of Mexico is the cold front and, associated with it, a strong, rotary wind field. These fronts usually propagate from northwest to southeast with a recurrence interval of 2-10 days. They occur most frequently from September through May in the northern Gulf of Mexico. Our earlier analyses showed that the sub-surface pressures and alongshore barotropic pressure gradients are usually highly coherent with the alongshore wind stress, especially throughout months characterized by recurrent cold front passage events. Therefore, it is also of interest to examine daily behavior of the pressure and the alongshore pressure gradient during these frontal passages.

Figure 18a depicts the wind field in the northwest Gulf of Mexico during January 1997. It is fairly typical of the autumn/winter wind behavior during cold front passage events. During the first three weeks of January 1997, there were three major cold front passage events beginning approximately on January 5, 11 and 16. The observed frontal winds were characterized by clockwise rotation with the winter storm events exhibiting winds with a strong southward component and more variable east/west wind component.

The response of the sub-surface pressure along the Louisiana-Texas coast to this wind field is depicted in Figure 18b. Similar to our previous observations and analyses, the sub-surface pressure was observed to be much more dependant on the alongshore wind component behavior. In spite of the very strong northerly wind component, which is expected to create set-down along this part of the coast, the opposite was observed. The first winter storm event was characterized by strong winds blowing from the northeast. Despite the strong offshore winds, sub-surface pressures increased across the study area from January 6-9, possibly as a result of downwelling created by the weaker easterly wind component A notable decrease of the sub-surface pressure along the coast was only observed when the offshore component of the wind was accompanied by an upcoast wind component (events on January 9-11 and 16-17, 1997). The upcoast wind stress lowered the pressure most probably as a result of upwelling dynamics.

The events of January 1997 are a good representation of autumn and winter wind/pressure relationships. Thus, the response of coastal sub-surface pressures to the wind field associated with cold front passages depends strongly on the alongshore wind component. When an upcoast wind stress is present, the pressure (water level) drops. However, if the frontal winds are accompanied by downcoast wind stress, pressure (water level) increases along the coast. The duration and magnitude of the pressure response were observed to be closely related to the duration and strength of the alongshore component of the wind stress.

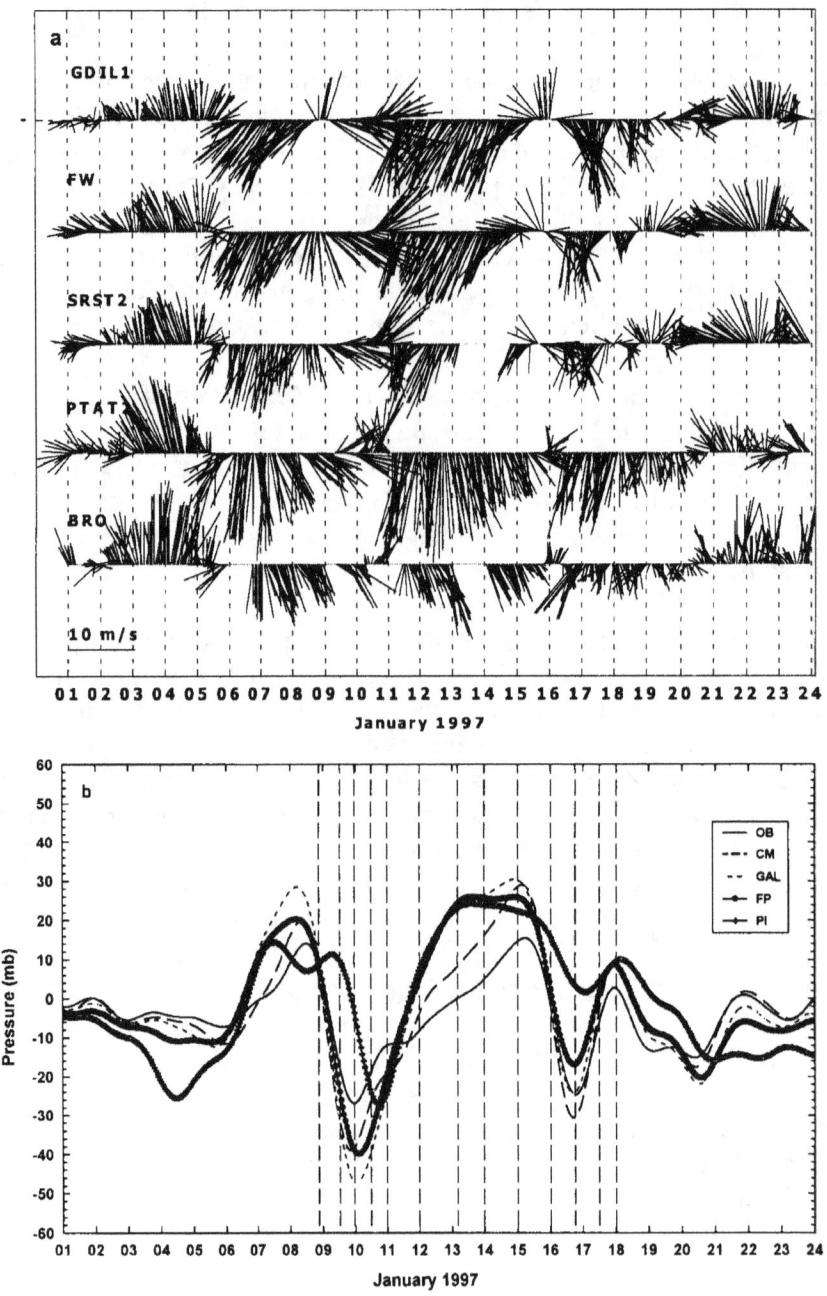

Figure 18. (a) Wind vectors across the study region for January 1997. The oceanographic convention is used for vector orientation(i.e. northward points to top of page); (b) Sub-surface pressures for five stations across the LATEX inner shelf in January 1997. The dashed lines in (a) indicate 0000h of each day. The dashed lines of (b) correspond with the time events shown in Figure 19.

28

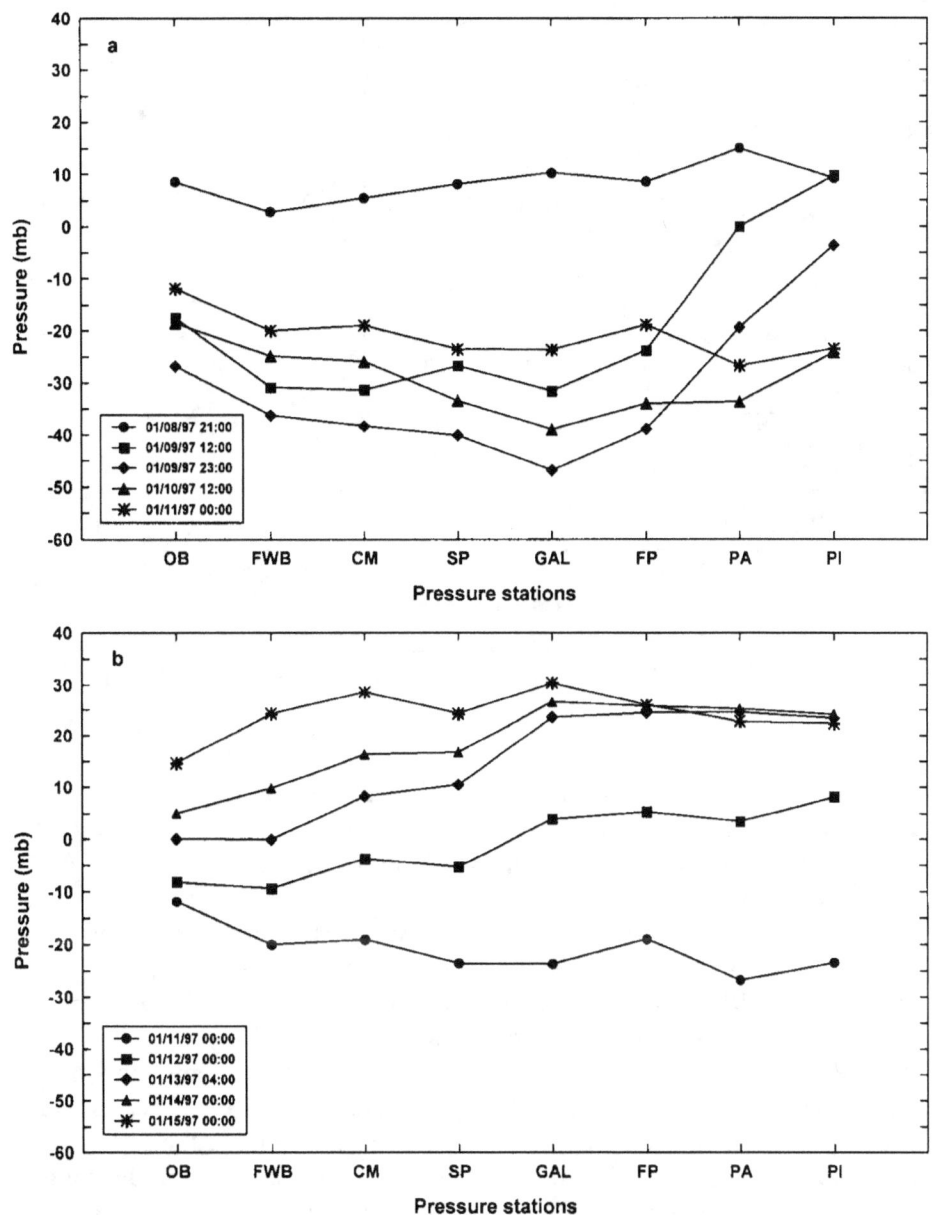

Figure 19. Sub-surface pressure measurements across the LATEX inner shelf for (a) January 8-11; (b) January 11-15; and (c) January 15-18, 1997 showing pressure changes and pressure gradient changes related to wind forcing.

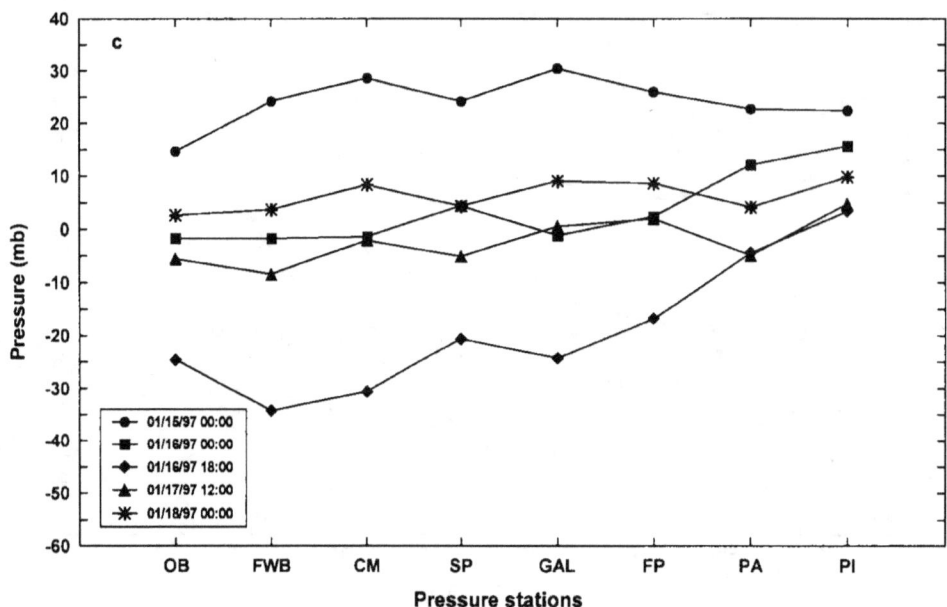

Figure 19 (continued). Sub-surface pressure measurements across the LATEX inner shelf for (a) January 8-11; (b) January 11-15; and (c) January 15-18, 1997 showing pressure changes and pressure gradient changes related to wind forcing.

Sub-surface pressure measurements along the Louisiana-Texas coast between January 8 and 18, 1997 are shown in Figure 19 (a-c). See Figure 18 for the wind and pressure conditions. These plots enable the investigation of changes in the barotropic pressure gradient that may be created by frontal winds across the inner shelf of the LATEX region. We begin the analysis on January 8 (Figure 19a, solid circles), with weakening northeasterly winds. At this time, coastal sub-surface pressures were relatively high and the pressure gradient along the coast was very weak. By January 9 (Figure 19a,   squares on graph) with a directional wind shift from downcoast to upcoast, coastal sub-surface pressures decreased by at least 30 mb. The alongshore pressure gradient had changed substantially with the development of a strong gradient along the Texas coast, between GAL and PI. Little pressure gradient was observed between FWB and GAL. Later on January 9 (Figure 19a, diamonds on graph), the pressure gradient along the Louisiana coast opposed that along the Texas coast. Such a gradient distribution (especially the opposing slopes along the northern and western part of the Gulf) generally persists as long as the upcoast wind component is active.

The second panel (Figure 19b) corresponded to a time period of winds from the northeast. It shows the pressure and pressure gradient changes that one usually observes when the alongshore wind component switches from upcoast to downcoast. Between January 11 (circles on graph) and January 14 (triangles on graph), sub-surface pressures increased 20-50 mb. Over that time, the pressure gradient changed from a weak pressure gradient along the entire LATEX inner shelf to a notable but rather gradual slope between OB and GAL, with lowest pressures along the LA coast and highest pressures along the TX coast.

The third panel (Figure 19c) depicts pressure and gradients from January 15-19, 1997, the second cold front passage event that started with upcoast wind stress, but shifted to downcoast wind stress after a day or so, depending on the station location. The pressure changes caused by the upcoast winds between January 15 (circles) and 16 (diamonds) were similar to those depicted in Figure 19a, however, the pressure gradient changes were less intense across the LATEX inner shelf. The less organized distribution of the alongshore barotropic pressure gradient coincided with a less organized wind field. Nevertheless, one may observe that this short-lived upcoast wind stress event created a well-defined pressure gradient between GAL and PI and a weaker but notable gradient from FWB to PI. Similar behavior of the alongshore gradient was observed for other analyzed cold front cases.

F. Evidence for Coastal-Trapped Waves

The 1996 summer time-series of the sub-surface pressure also revealed the existence of long period oscillations. They were observed at all analyzed pressure gauge and water level stations along the Louisiana-Texas coast (Figure 20). These long period oscillations were most evident between July 11 and August 19, 1996. Their period was about 10 days and their amplitudes varied from one place and event to another but, on average, they were at least 10 mb. During the same time period, similar long period fluctuations were also present in atmospheric pressure and alongshore wind component time series along the Louisiana-Texas coast. Figure 21 shows the recorded fluctuations of the atmospheric and sub-surface pressure, and alongshore wind observed at Freshwater Bayou. Both atmospheric pressure and wind display well-defined low frequency motion with periods of about 10 days and amplitudes, on average, of 5 mb and 6 m/s, respectively. In addition, such long period fluctuations were simultaneously observed in the alongshore current series at the mooring line off Cameron, LA (see Figure 15b). The spatial vastness of the pressure events as well as the time lag among the recorded series (which can be seen in Figure 22), may suggest that these are long coastal-trapped waves. They move westward along the Louisiana coast and then southward along the Texas coast. They were probably forced by fluctuating atmospheric pressure and/or wind. However, to accept or reject this hypothesis one needs to perform more sophisticated analyses.

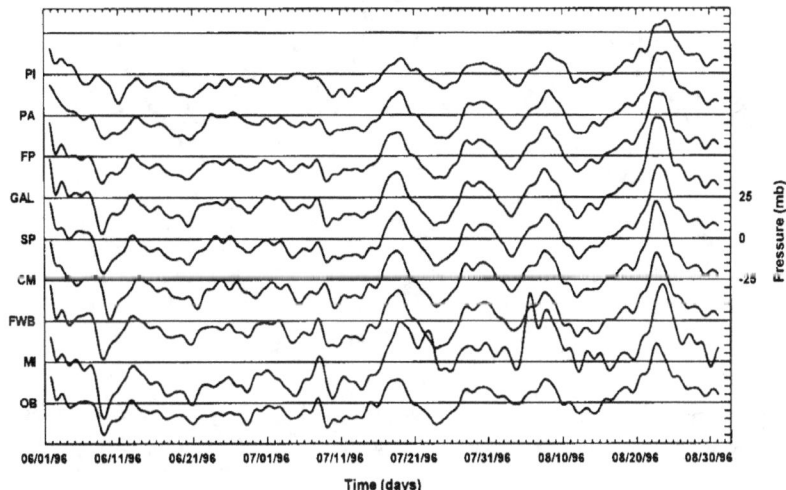

Figure 20. Sub-surface pressure (de-meaned, low-pass filtered) at all coastal stations between June 1 and August 30, 1996.

31

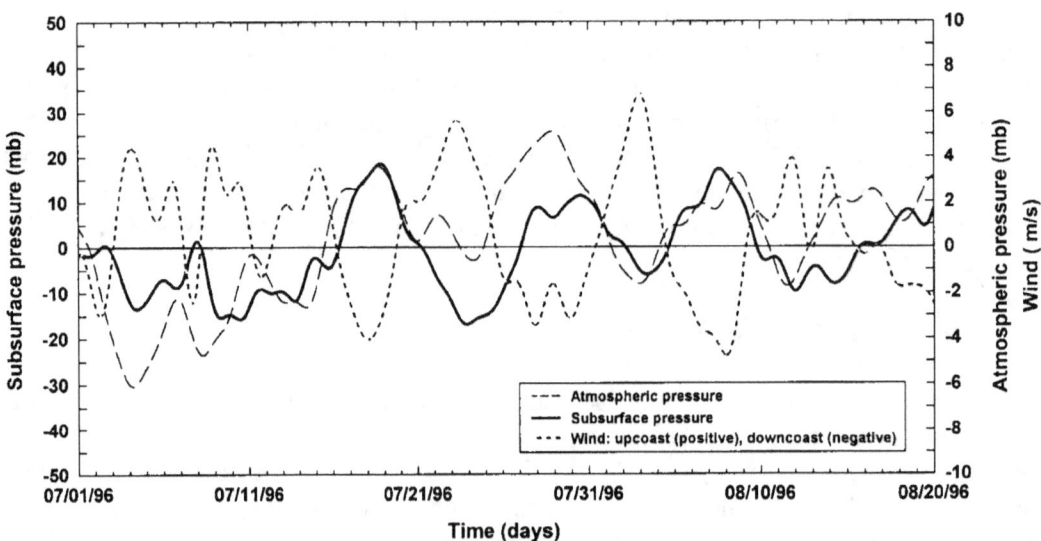

Figure 21. Sub-surface pressure, atmospheric pressure, and the alongshore wind component velocity at Freshwater Bayou from July 1 through August 19, 1996.

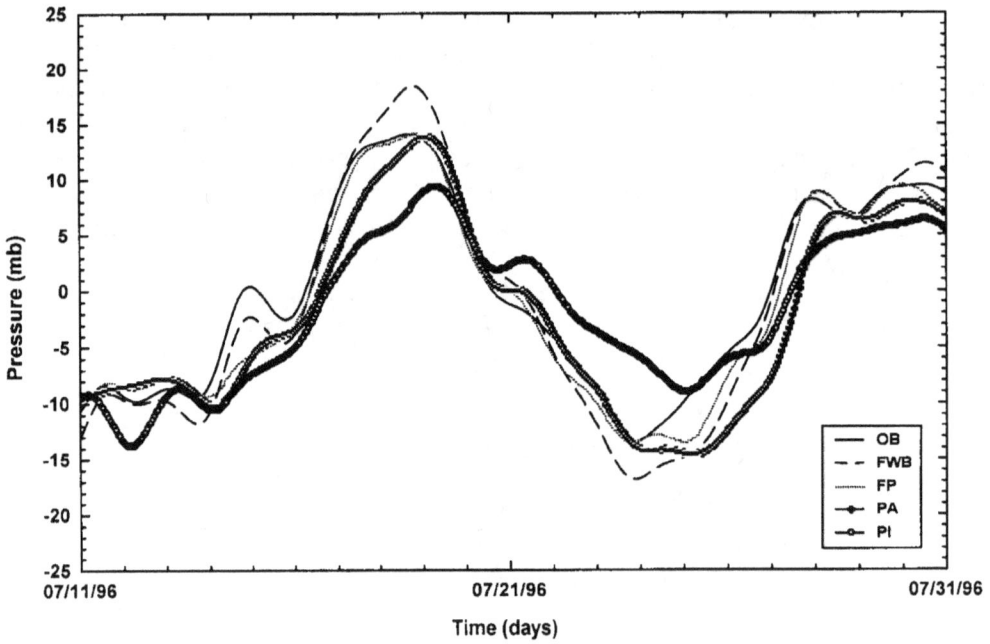

Figure 22. Sub-surface pressure at five coastal stations between July 11 and July 31, 1996, showing the timing of the sub-surface pressure peaks and troughs, perhaps indicative of a coastal-trapped wave.

Possible existence of coastal-trapped waves on the Louisiana-Texas shelf was first discussed by Current (1996). She employed a wind –forced coastal-trapped wave model to study subinertial circulation on this shelf and summarized that the wind-forced coastal-trapped waves

32

were responsible for a substantial fraction of this circulation, especially during winter months when these waves were excited by winds associated with cold front passages. However, the model performance decreased in summer months, especially in July and August, and this was attributed to the fact that the wind forcing was weak and baroclinic effects were more dominant. Based on data rather than the model, she also identified free continental shelf waves that formed near Atchafalaya Bay, LA by Hurricane Andrew and propagated as far south as the Rio Grande, TX.

Our data suggest that, even in summer, the coastal-trapped waves may play a significant role in the shelf circulation. These long-period fluctuations dominated the current and subsurface pressure subinertial signals, especially evident between mid-July and mid-August, 1996. Results from an empirical orthogonal function analysis obtained form a spectral matrix suggest that the pressure fluctuations are forced by wind and/or atmospheric pressure on the Louisiana shelf (there is a very small time lag between the subsurface pressure stations there) and then they propagate southward along the Texas coast with the phase speed of ~ 6 m/s.

IV. SUMMARY AND CONCLUSIONS

A semi-annual cycle in sub-surface pressure/water level was detected in the monthly mean pressure data along the Louisiana and Texas inner shelves. Mean monthly pressure maxima were measured in October of each year with secondary maxima in April/May. The pressure minima were observed most often in January/February with secondary minima in July/June. These seasonal pressure changes were closely associated with seasonal changes in alongshore wind forcing. Pressure minima coincided with relatively strong upcoast wind stress and pressure maxima coincided with relatively strong downcoast wind stress. Strong westward wind stresses were measured in October and again in April/May. Along the Louisiana coast, the October winds had an offshore component whereas in April/May wind stress had an onshore component, indicating the over-riding importance of the alongshore component of the wind. A semi-annual coastal water level signal was discussed previously for coastal stations in the Gulf of Mexico by Whitaker (1971) and Sturges and Blaha (1976) and attributed to thermally induced changes, wind stress changes and river discharge. Our results indicate that the coastal water level changes were most closely associated with changes in the direction (sign) of the alongshore wind stress.

A more detailed analysis of the water level fluctuations on the synoptic scale revealed that the highs and lows in water levels were attributed to one or more distinct wind events within each month. Westward (Louisiana) and southwestward (Texas) wind stress events produced the highest coastal water levels. Lowest water levels along the Texas coast were produced by northward wind stress. Along the Louisiana coast, lowest water levels occurred in close association with strong eastward wind stress. Although similarity in water level responses were observable in the water level records, there were events for which the coastal water levels across the region responded differently to a wind event. The change in coastline orientation from Louisiana to Texas in relationship to wind stress produced interesting differences in water level responses on the synoptic scale. For example, a strong wind blowing towards the east along the Louisiana coast produced alongshore wind stress, upwelling and a reduction in coastal water levels due to Ekman set-down. This same wind stress along the Texas coast resulted in cross-shelf offshore wind and little water level change.

Statistical analyses of the relationships between pressure and wind stress revealed that at all stations and in both summer and winter seasons, highest coherences were observed between the alongshore wind stress and sub-surface pressure variations. Along the Louisiana coast, coherences of 0.7-0.8 were found between pressure and alongshore wind stress at frequencies between 2 and 20 days. No large seasonal differences were observed in the levels of coherence between pressure and alongshore wind stress along the Louisiana coast. There was some evidence from the available data that, along the Louisiana coast, the maximum coherences between pressure and alongshore wind stress were at lower frequencies during winter. The coherences between pressure and cross-shore wind stress were low in comparison with the alongshore wind stress results. Along the Louisiana coast, the variances explained by the cross-shore wind stresses were notably higher during winter than during summer and at shorter periods. At Oyster Bayou and Freshwater Bayou, near Atchafalaya Bay, coherences between cross-shore wind stress and pressure were as high as 0.7 in the 2-4 day period during winter. Walker and Hammack (2000) demonstrated that winds blowing from the northwest are the most efficient at flushing water levels from the bays. Average water level changes in the Vermilion-Atchafalaya Bay region during cold front passages are typically 1 meter (Kemp et al., 1980; Walker and Hammack, 2000). The increase in offshore wind events during the October through March time period could explain this high frequency response to cross-shore wind forcing. The results of Chuang and Wiseman (1983) indicate that water levels within Atchafalaya Bay respond more to cross-shore wind forcing than to alongshore wind forcing, due to the shallow depths in the bay and on the inner shelf seaward of it. Our results are not directly comparable with theirs as they chose north/south and east/west vector orientations rather than alongshore and cross-shore orientations. Our results indicate that coastal water levels in the Atchafalaya Bay region exhibit responses to both alongshore and cross-shore wind stress during winter, albeit at different time intervals.

Along the Texas coast, coherences between pressure and alongshore wind stress were also much higher than those with cross-shore wind stress. Coherences between alongshore wind stress and pressure were 0.7 to 0.8 during winter and 0.48 to 0.70 during summer. The highest cross-shore coherences (0.3-0.72) were observed between 3 and 8 days and did not exhibit distinct seasonal variations as they did along the Louisiana coast.

The analysis of alongshore pressure gradients and wind forcing revealed coherences above 0.6 in summer and above 0.8 in winter for some station pairs along the Louisiana and Texas coasts. Seasonal differences were more pronounced along the Louisiana coast. Analysis of graphical outputs showed that the pressure gradients between the Louisiana stations and between Louisiana and Texas stations were probably a direct response to the wind forcing. For example, westward (alongshore) wind stress resulted in negative pressure gradients along the Louisiana coastline (eastern stations-western stations). The highest coherences along the Louisiana coast were observed between Oyster Bayou (east of Atchafalaya Bay) and other stations (west of Atchafalaya Bay), suggesting perhaps that the low density plume of freshwater discharged from the bay may serve to enhance pressure gradients along this portion of the coast.

Current meter measurements on the inner shelf near Cameron (Murray et al., in preparation) were compared with the pressure gradients along the Louisiana-Texas continental shelf. Visual inspection of graphical outputs revealed similarities between pressure gradients along the Texas coast and flow off Cameron. Further statistical investigation demonstrated the existence of significant relationships only during summer. This is an important result as it indicates that inner shelf currents along at least a portion of the Louisiana shelf during summer may be driven by pressure gradients and currents generated along the Texas coast.

In general, however, the computed pressure gradients were consistent with gradients that would result from the wind stress forcing. Based on this study, we conclude that the barotropic pressure gradients along the coast do not provide a major control on current variability except in the west portion of the study region during the summer. Further investigation of this is warranted, however, as simultaneous measurements of currents and sub-surface pressure along the LATEX shelf are still scarce.

A detailed analysis of pressure/water level fluctuations along the Louisiana/Texas coastline was performed for January 1997. This analysis demonstrated that water levels only fall when winds blow upcoast. Thus, the presence of strong winter winds from the northeast does not reduce coastal water levels, but increases them. Thus, all frontal passages do not have the same effect on coastal water levels. Winter storms that blow upcoast (west winds) have a much stronger flushing effect in coastal Louisiana than winds blowing downcoast (east winds).

Long period oscillations in pressure/water level were detected along the Louisiana-Texas coastline during the 1996 summer. They exhibited periods of about 10 days and amplitudes of at least 10 mb. Similar long-period oscillations were evident in the corresponding atmospheric pressure and alongshore component of the wind stress. The spatial vastness of the pressure events and the time lag between stations may suggest that these are long coastal-trapped waves. Current (1996) observed similar long-period coastal-trapped waves in her model results, however, they were best developed in winter. Further more sophisticated analyses are needed to better understand the forcing mechanisms and behavior of these relatively long-period water level fluctuations.

V. REFERENCES

Bendat. J.S. and A.G. Piersol. 1986. Random Data: Analysis and Measurement Procedures. Second edition, John Wiley and Sons. 566 pp.

Brown, W.S. and J.D. Irish. 1987. A description of subtidal pressure field observations on the northern California continental shelf during the coastal ocean dynamics experiment. Journal of Geophysical Research 92(C2):1605-1635.

Brown, W.S., N.R. Pettigrew and J.D. Irish. 1985. The Nantucket shoals flux experiment (NSFE79), Part II: The structure and variability of across-shelf pressure gradients. Journal of Physical Oceanography 15(6):749-771.

Chuang, W.S. and W.J. Wiseman. 1983. Coastal sea level response to frontal passages on the Louisiana-Texas shelf. Journal of Geophysical Research 88:2,615-2,620.

Cochrane, J.D. and F.J. Kelley. 1986. Low-frequency circulation on the Texas-Louisiana continental shelf. Journal of Geophysical Research 91:10,645-10,659.

Crout, R.L., W.J. Wiseman, Jr., and W.S. Chuang. 1984. Variability of wind-driven currents, west Louisiana inner continental shelf. Contributions to Marine Science 27:1-11.

Csanady, G.T. 1982. Circulation in the coastal ocean. D. Reidel, Hingham, MA. 279 pp.

Current, C.L. 1996. Spectral model simulation of wind driven subinertial circulation on the inner Texas-Louisiana shelf. PhD Dissertation. Texas A&M University, College Station, TX. 144 pp.

DiMego, G.J., L.F. Bosart, and G.W. Endersen. 1976. An examination of the frequency and mean conditions surrounding frontal incursions into the Gulf of Mexico and Caribbean. Mon. Weather Rev. 104:709-718.

Jarosz, E., S.P. Murray, P.S. Niiler, E.T. Weeks, and C.E. Ebbesmeyer. 1996. Comparison of ADCP and drifter observations of circulation in the Louisiana-Texas coastal current, summer 1994, *EOS,* Transactions, American Geophysical Union. 76(3):OS98, Ocean Sciences Conference, San Diego, CA.

Hsu, S.A. 1988. Coastal meteorology. San Diego, CA: Academic Press, Inc. 260 pp.

Kemp, G.P., J.T. Wells, and I.Ll. van Heerden. 1980. Frontal passages affect delta development in Louisiana. Coastal Oceanography and Climatology News 3:4-5.

Large, W.G. and S.Pond. 1981. Open ocean momentum flux measurements in moderate and strong winds. Journal of Physical Oceanography 11:324-336.

Lentz, S.J. The Amazon River plume during AMASSEDS: Subtidal current variability and the importance of wind forcing. Journal of Geophysical Research 100(C2):2377-2390.

Lewis, J.K. and R.O. Reid. 1985. Local wind forcing of a coastal sea at subinertial frequencies. Journal of Geophysical Research 90:934-944.

Marmorino, G.O. 1982. Wind-forced sea level variability along the west Florida shelf (Winter, 1978). Journal of Physical Oceanography 12:389-405.

Milliman, J.D. and R.H. Meade. 1983. World-wide delivery of river sediment to the ocean. Journal of Geology 91:1-21.

Murray, S.P., E. Jarosz, and E.T. Weeks. 1998. Physical oceanographic observations of the coastal plume. In: Murray, S.P. (editor). An observational study of the Mississippi-Atchafalaya coastal plume; Final Report, OCS Study MMS 98-0040. U.S. Dept. of the Interior, Minerals Mgmt. Service, Gulf of Mexico OCS Region, New Orleans, LA. 513 pp.

Murray, S.P., E. Jarosz, and E.T. Weeks. In preparation. Velocity and transport characteristics of the Louisiana-Texas coastal current; final report. U.S. Dept. of the Interior, Minerals Mgmt. Service, Gulf of Mexico OCS Region, New Orleans, LA. 91 pp.

Smith, N.P. 1978. Low-frequency reversals of nearshore currents in the north-western Gulf of Mexico. Contributions to Marine Science 21:103-115.

Sturges, W. and J.P. Blaha. 1976. A western boundary current in the Gulf of Mexico. Science 192:367-369.

Walker, N.D., A. Hammack, R. Cunningham, and H.H. Roberts. 1997. Satellite observations of circulation, sediment distribution and transport in the Atchafalaya-Vermilion Bay System; final report. U.S. Army Corps of Engineers, Waterways Experiment Station, Vicksburg, MS. 88 pp.

Walker, N.D. and A. Hammack. 2000. Impacts of winter storms on circulation and sediment transport: Atchafalaya-Vermilion Bay Region, Louisiana, U.S.A. Journal of Coastal Research 16:996-1010.

Walker, N.D. 2001. Wind and eddy related circulation on the Louisiana/Texas shelf and slope determined from satellite and in-situ measurements; October 1993-August 1994. OCS Study MMS 2001-025. U.S. Dept. of the Interior, Minerals Mgmt. Service, Gulf of Mexico OCS Region, New Orleans, LA. 58 pp.

Whitaker, R.E. 1971. Seasonal variations of steric and recorded sea level of the Gulf of Mexico. M.S. Thesis, Texas A&M University, College Station, TX. 111 pp.

Wiseman, W.J., Jr. and F.J. Kelly. 1994. Salinity variability within the Louisiana coastal current during 1982 flood season. Estuaries 17:732-739.

The Department of the Interior Mission

As the Nation's principal conservation agency, the Department of the Interior has responsibility for most of our nationally owned public lands and natural resources. This includes fostering sound use of our land and water resources; protecting our fish, wildlife, and biological diversity; preserving the environmental and cultural values of our national parks and historical places; and providing for the enjoyment of life through outdoor recreation. The Department assesses our energy and mineral resources and works to ensure that their development is in the best interests of all our people by encouraging stewardship and citizen participation in their care. The Department also has a major responsibility for American Indian reservation communities and for people who live in island territories under U.S. administration.

The Minerals Management Service Mission

As a bureau of the Department of the Interior, the Minerals Management Service's (MMS) primary responsibilities are to manage the mineral resources located on the Nation's Outer Continental Shelf (OCS), collect revenue from the Federal OCS and onshore Federal and Indian lands, and distribute those revenues.

Moreover, in working to meet its responsibilities, the **Offshore Minerals Management Program** administers the OCS competitive leasing program and oversees the safe and environmentally sound exploration and production of our Nation's offshore natural gas, oil and other mineral resources. The MMS **Minerals Revenue Management** meets its responsibilities by ensuring the efficient, timely and accurate collection and disbursement of revenue from mineral leasing and production due to Indian tribes and allottees, States and the U.S. Treasury.

The MMS strives to fulfill its responsibilities through the general guiding principles of: (1) being responsive to the public's concerns and interests by maintaining a dialogue with all potentially affected parties and (2) carrying out its programs with an emphasis on working to enhance the quality of life for all Americans by lending MMS assistance and expertise to economic development and environmental protection.